'This is a wonderfully refresh
which conveys her spiritual toughness and the
freedom she found through reflecting on the cross of Christ. For those who associate Julian only with her vision of the hazelnut, this will be a revelation.'
Angela Tilby, canon emeritus, Christ Church, Oxford

'I absolutely love this book. As the foreword explains, it aims to draw the reader into a profoundly meditative encounter with Julian's visions and understanding of God. It manages this with a beautiful simplicity that will draw in any reader. Informed by the author's deep scholarship, this a sure and reliable guide.'
Santha Bhattacharji, fellow emeritus, St Benet's Hall, University of Oxford, and president, Churches Fellowship for Psychical and Spiritual Studies

'Emma Pennington has opened the writings of Julian of Norwich to us in a fresh and wonderful way. She has also given us, in this book, a spiritual treasure which causes us to journey and explore and, in that quest, to venture deeper and deeper into the love of God, with Julian as our companion.'
Robert Willis, dean of Canterbury Cathedral

'Emma Pennington has that rare gift of bringing theological and literary insights together. She transports us to a different world – Julian's world of the 14th century – and yet makes it completely and profoundly accessible to the modern reader. This is a very moving book, one to be read slowly and reflected on deeply. With all its discomforts, as well as comfort, may I encourage you to accept her and Julian's invitations to come and stand at the foot of Christ's cross.'
Colin Fletcher OBE, Bishop of Dorchester

The Bible Reading Fellowship
15 The Chambers, Vineyard
Abingdon OX14 3FE
brf.org.uk

The Bible Reading Fellowship (BRF) is a Registered Charity (233280)

ISBN 978 0 85746 519 1
First published 2020
10 9 8 7 6 5 4 3 2 1 0
All rights reserved

Text © Emma Pennington 2020
This edition © The Bible Reading Fellowship 2020
Cover image © PjrWindows / Alamy Stock Photo

The author asserts the moral right to be identified as the author of this work

Acknowledgements
Unless otherwise acknowledged, scripture quotations are taken from The New Revised Standard Version of the Bible, Anglicised edition, copyright © 1989, 1995 by the Division of Christian Education of the National Council of the Churches of Christ in the United States of America. Used by permission. All rights reserved.

Scripture quotations marked NASB are taken from the New American Standard Bible, Copyright © 1960, 1962, 1963, 1968, 1971, 1972, 1973, 1975, 1977, 1995 by The Lockman Foundation. Used by permission. (**Lockman.org**).

Image acknowledgements listed on pp. 7–8.

Every effort has been made to trace and contact copyright owners for material used in this resource. We apologise for any inadvertent omissions or errors, and would ask those concerned to contact us so that full acknowledgement can be made in the future.

A catalogue record for this book is available from the British Library

Printed and bound by CPI Group (UK) Ltd, Croydon CR0 4YY

EMMA PENNINGTON

AT THE FOOT OF THE CROSS *with* JULIAN OF NORWICH

For God's lovers

Photocopying for churches

Please report to CLA Church Licence any photocopy you make from this publication. Your church administrator or secretary will know who manages your CLA Church Licence.

The information you need to provide to your CLA Church Licence administrator is as follows:

Title, Author, Publisher and ISBN

If your church doesn't hold a CLA Church Licence, information about obtaining one can be found at **uk.ccli.com**

CONTENTS

LIST OF PLATES

between pages 96 and 97

Preface

I was standing in a circle with about 30 other women. Although we had spent all day together on a training course, we still shuffled in our skins, feeling exposed under each other's flickering gaze. For we had come to a moment in the day, a final moment, which had been tantalisingly held before us as an experience that would empower and enliven each one of us. Nervously we waited for instructions. It was with some relief that our leader and guru invited us to turn to our right. No longer burdened by embarrassment, a sigh softened the room; the worst was surely over. We were then asked gently to place the palm of our hand between the shoulder blades of the person in front of us. After a little shifting and pardoning, the circle tightened as we bound ourselves into one entity. It felt strange, a tickling sensation, and yet at the same time this unseen touch compelled me to relinquish my hard-won independence and join the circle. A horror rippled through me when, in this position, we were then asked to name out loud the women who have been the most significant and influential figures in our lives. As my turn came nearer and nearer, my mind emptied more and more. Who should I say? Who has been influential? My mother, of course, my sister… surely they are not the only women in my life? Who else? Oh no, what are their names? What if I get them wrong, muddled up like so much of my memory? Will I be corrected or laughed at? I'll say nothing. Through my panic I began to hear a single name, repeated again and again by those who stood around me. Surely they don't mean… Yes, it must be… Julian.

Like those around me, Julian has been one of the most influential women in my life, and like so many, it is her voice that has been woven into my history. I was first introduced to her at Exeter University, when I was reading English and Medieval Studies. It was in the second year, when we were studying the rather intimidatingly entitled 'Medieval religious writing', that Julian and her fellow mystics came to my attention. I had never read such powerful and overwhelming texts before. Even through their Middle English I was inspired and transformed by their words of God. They opened a door; more than a door – a vision and a desire that overwhelmed me. As a passionate and somewhat romantic 19-year-old, I began to consume the spiritual classics, sought out those who lived the contemplative life and dedicated myself to God. Among all the writings that inspired and guided me – Augustine, Richard Rolle, Walter Hilton, Margery Kempe, the author of *The Cloud of Unknowing*, John of the Cross, Teresa of Ávila, Gregory of Nyssa and so on – it was Julian who lingered most. Time and again I read her words, wrote on her, preached on her and quoted her, but somehow the essence of her words was always intangible and beyond my grasp. Yet each time her texts somehow drew me into an even deeper awareness of the presence and mystery of God.

It was with great joy that, in my mid-30s, I was given the opportunity to study her writings with some of the greatest Julian scholars of our day and weekly immerse myself in the language and multiple meanings of her words. Throughout the ten years it took me to complete my doctoral thesis, Julian's voice continually led me through scholarly discipline and analysis to encounter and prayer. In this book I seek to share with you this experience of encountering God through Julian's words, crystallised within a medieval text. I aim to bring you to that place of encounter through a detailed exploration of Julian's use of language and images, which describe her visions of the cross. This is the beginning of an encounter with her text that seeks to enable you to come to your own place of prayer and contemplation.

Introduction

ENCOUNTERING JULIAN'S WRITTEN WORDS

How is it that a woman from the late 14th century, about whom we know hardly anything at all, comes to be named time and again as one of the most influential figures in some people's lives today? The answer to this question is not necessarily found in history books. There is only one that makes a specific reference to Julian: Margery Kempe's account of her visit to Julian is the only definitive external evidence we have of her historic identity. Who she was, what she was like and how she lived her life are questions that neither history nor her writings can easily answer. It is through the manuscripts of her writings that Julian's voice has spoken directly to so many in this age. However, these writings do not help us to draw an accurate picture of Julian the person. Sadly, they contain no colourful life history interwoven within her words or neat biography to enlighten us. Instead, the person Julian continually evades our gaze, as she frustratingly insists on hiding behind and within her writings. All we can definitely state from her texts, biographically speaking, is that she had a revelatory experience in 1373 which arose from a serious illness; that she was an anchoress attached to St Julian's Church in Norwich; that she wrote two texts based on her experience; and that locally, at least, she held some sort of reputation for her revelations. The rest is conjecture and surmise, however convincing the detective work might be. Yet it is through these same writings, often called *Revelations of Divine Love*, that Julian has spoken so profoundly to so many in this age, making her one of our most influential women.

It is Julian the writer who, through her accounts, descriptions, musings, explanations, reasoning, imagination, ideas, devotion and love, creates a chamber, a liminal space, in which we are invited to step, not to find her but to encounter God. As Julian herself says, 'As for the showing it only makes me good if I love God better, and in as much as you love God better it is more to you than to me' (*Revelations of Divine Love*, ch. 9, lines 1–2). Julian cannot recreate her experience or simulate a mystical encounter for us, but she can take us to the threshold of the ineffable through the use of our faculties and emotions, thereby enabling us to enter an awareness of the divine presence. This book is therefore not about Julian's life, however intriguing that may be, nor does it seek to expound her thinking, despite its illuminating profundity. Instead, it is a work that invites you to enter into the substance and language of Julian's words, to hear her voice, which speaks to us amid the crackles of time and calls us to stand with her at the foot of the cross so we may know and love God the better.

In order to enter more deeply into Julian's written word, we first need to consider what kind of texts Julian has left for us, and the answer to that question begins with where they came from. What is it that Julian writes? The modern extracts, translations, summaries and editions which first introduced Julian to us all flow from five vellum manuscripts held in various libraries in Britain and France. The oldest dates from the 15th century and gathers together a number of different works about the life of prayer. Embedded among these so-called devotional texts can be found what today is commonly referred to as the short version of Julian's work. We cannot say for sure when it was written, but most people agree that this was Julian's first edition of her work. It has the feel of an initial documentation of her visions and her early reflections on them, thus it is often dated to the early 1380s. The other version of her writing is much longer and hence is referred to as the long text. Julian intimated that she spent just under 20 years reflecting deeply on what she saw and experienced on that night in 1373. So it seems reasonable to place the long text at least 20 years after her visionary experience. None of the manuscripts gives us a clear title page, necessitating the need for scholars to invent a title for both texts. These have varied in time, depending on editorial preference, but now they are generally referred to as *Revelations of Divine Love* for the long text and *The Visions of Julian of Norwich* for the short text, or simply 'the short text'.

Sadly, we do not have Julian's original manuscript of either the short or the long texts. We only have copies of copies, some dating to as late as the 17th century. Scholars have tried to remove the layers of interpretation and modernising that have accumulated over the years, as if there were some original masterpiece hidden underneath just waiting to be revealed. But even painstaking comparisons between the different manuscripts have failed to recover a definitive original or authentic version. One of the reasons why it is so hard to discern an original text from the accretions of time, apart from the human errors that slip in during the copying of the text, is that past scribes and editors approached a person's writing in a very different way from how we do today. There was not the same sense of authorship or even intellectual property. Rather, scribes saw it as their task to update the spelling, add structure to the original work or even give explanations so that a later audience could understand it more easily. In each case the importance of copying the text did not so much lie in the preservation of an original work but in enabling the sense and heart of Julian's writing to be as accessible and helpful to the reader as possible. Modern books of extracts and loose translations of Julian's writings seek to do much the same today, and this is often the way in which Julian's work and ideas have predominantly become known by a wide-ranging audience.

Defining *Revelations of Divine Love*

As anyone who has picked up or been given a complete copy of Julian's *Revelations of Divine Love* will quickly discover, it is not exactly a light summer read. The wonderful paragraphs and phrases we have come to know so well are all there, but they are embedded like shining pennies within a dense and rich mix of ingredients. It is this complex blend of visionary narrative, interpretation, mysticism, theology and devotional encounter, all expressed in unfamiliar Middle English words that transmute and intertwine with each other in their meaning and expression, which makes Julian's *Revelations of Divine Love* not only difficult to read but also impossible to define. Her text simply refuses to fit neatly into any of the categories of visionary, mystical or theological work we might try to give it. So what kind of a text has Julian left us? This is an important question, because how we approach a text often has more of a bearing on how we understand it than we might imagine.

A visionary work

On the face of it, Julian writes a simple document that describes the series of visions she had in 1373 – hence the choice by one of the earliest editors of the text, Edmund Colledge and James Walsh, to call their edition *A Book of Showings*, a descriptive title that denotes Julian's text as a series of visions or showings. However, when compared with equivalent visionary works of the 14th century, it is clear just how different Julian's so-called visionary work is.

Just up the road from Norwich, in King's Lynn, a somewhat colourful character, Margery Kempe, was compiling a book of her own visionary experiences at the same time as Julian. In a way her *Book of Margery Kempe* is a defence of her extraordinary life, but, interwoven with this biography, Margery gives us detailed descriptions of her visionary experiences, in which she imaginatively enters the world of the gospels and intimately shares in the life of Jesus. In one vision Mary hands her the baby Jesus for her to wash and place in the crib straight after he has been born. Sometimes Margery's visionary participation was rather overwhelming for those around her. Any image of the cross could cause her to break out into such wailing and weeping that she had to be taken from the church. The text Margery wrote can clearly be defined as a visionary work and follows a form of visionary writing from the 13th and 14th centuries that was predominantly found in the Low Countries.

Julian's writings describe a vision of the events of the Passion, but unlike her visionary contemporaries she did not get emotionally or affectively involved in what she saw. We do not get the sense from her text that she played a role within the narrative of her visions. Instead, Julian stood apart in the more liminal space of observing and interpreting what she saw. Julian did write a visionary work, but somehow this title does not seem to do justice to the extraordinary words that then flow from what she saw.

A mystical work

Ever since Julian's words emerged from their vellum resting places in the 1900s, early editors and scholars have described her writing as a mystical text. Today the term 'mystical' has many different meanings, from union with the divine to altered states of consciousness. Primarily, however, in modern parlance it defines a work that haltingly seeks to articulate an ineffable experience of God in all his mystery. The strange account that Paul gives in 2 Corinthians is seen as the archetypal mystical experience:

> I know a person in Christ who fourteen years ago was caught up to the third heaven – whether in the body or out of the body I do not know; God knows. And I know that such a person – whether in the body or out of the body I do not know; God knows – was caught up into Paradise and heard things that are not to be told, that no mortal is permitted to repeat.
>
> 2 CORINTHIANS 12:2–4

Paul tries to describe an event that is ultimately a mystery. He speaks in a halting manner and is unable to articulate exactly what was going on or what was heard when in this state; it is both hidden and secret. Yet at the same time there is a grounding of this experience in the words of scripture: both 'third heaven' and the prohibition to speak are rooted in the biblical tradition of apocalyptic writing found in Ezekiel, Baruch and even the gospels.

Julian similarly describes an experience which happened to her in 1373, when the crucifix that was held before her eyes took on a ‘common’ light. The subsequent visions of the cross and the description that flows from this event soon spread out into a delta of ideas and even instruction that, especially in the long version of her writing, leaves the mystical experience far behind.

A theological treatise

As Julian’s writings have become better known, commentators have come to recognise the profound thinking that makes up much of the body of her work and, as a result, they have sought to identify Julian’s texts as a theological treatise and Julian herself as a theologian.

Julian and her texts rightly deserve this heightened respect and the notoriety within the theology faculties that this inadvertently brings. However, any idea that one can easily distil from her complex interplay of language a cohesive theology of sin, or an ecological thesis from a single hazelnut, soon becomes a highly selective and mind-twisting process. I could try to summarise what Julian says on the Trinity or on sin, but Julian was not writing, or even intending to write, a theological treatise that expounded well-thought-out doctrines. She is not an Augustine or even an Aquinas, so trying to read her work as such just doesn’t work. That’s why you don’t find the most interesting research on Julian happening in most theology departments. Instead, it is to the English department you must go.

A literary masterpiece

It is invariably from the many hundreds of books and articles that emanate from a literary approach to Julian that you will find some of the richest and deepest insights on Julian’s words, and it is the literary world that has made her Middle English manuscripts accessible to us today. For it is here that you will find people approaching her work as a piece of crafted engagement, which utilises the devotional and theological landscape of the 14th century to draw the reader into experiencing, for themselves and through her words, what it was that she saw and later came to understand about God and our relationship with him.

Through a literary approach, you will find an appreciation of the nuances and intricacies of Julian's text. Single, simple and everyday words will change and transmute within her writing until they have a powerful theological meaning of their own. Approaching Julian's *Revelations of Divine Love* as a literary masterpiece does not necessarily strip it down through overzealous analysis to its bare bones of form and structure, but it allows the words to speak for themselves, so that we can listen for the voice of Julian coming through her words across the airwaves of time and interpretation.

A devotional invitation

So how are we to approach this text, which defies any simple labelling and refuses to fit into the mould of expectation? When Julian's text first came to public attention at the beginning of the 20th century, it was grouped together with a series of remarkable late 14th-century writings: *The Scale of Perfection* by Walter Hilton; an anonymous work now referred to as *The Cloud of Unknowing*; the writings of Richard Rolle; *The Book of Margery Kempe*. Together they are often given the modern label 'the English Mystics', though at first sight there seems to be very little to link them together as people: Hilton was an Augustinian canon at Thurgarten; we know very little about the *Cloud* author, but it is thought he may have been a member of the Carthusian order; Rolle was a hermit; Kempe was an unconventional visionary who defied the church authorities; and, finally, Julian was an enclosed anchoress committed to a life of prayer in a room attached to St Julian's Church in Norwich.

Yet each, in their own way, wrote to enable others on their search for a deeper knowledge of God. The *Cloud* author, Hilton and Rolle all wrote guides to help women who had devoted themselves to a life set apart in prayer: the enclosed and religious contemplatives. Kempe's book is as much a witness and testimony to the life of a lay woman dedicated to God as it is a visionary work. And Julian's work, while centred around a series of visions of the cross, is intimate in its devotional sharing of the meditations and explanations which arose from them. What brings this eclectic mix of texts together, however, is not necessarily the nature of the writers or even the content of their texts; it is how they have to date come to be used, read and made accessible to a wider public audience.

Each of these works was written at a remarkable time, much like our own, when the search to know God intimately and the hunger for wisdom and guidance on the spiritual path and life of prayer stemmed from the increasingly literate lay section of society as well as the traditional clerics and religious. The writings of both Rolle and Hilton were adapted to meet the demands of this growing group of devout people, most of whom could not read but would gather round a priest or rich friend to hear the expensive vellum books read out loud. Julian also updated her short text and, in the later version, directed her words to 'mine even cristen' rather than those only living the contemplative life. This small alteration suggests a desire by ordinary people to hear more of the wisdom and guidance that Julian would undoubtedly have spoken at her anchorhold window. Along with the other English Mystics, Julian has been preserved, written out in each age, hidden and treasured not just because hers is a visionary work, mystical text, theological treatise or literary masterpiece, but also because it has enabled someone, or some community, to know God better. For this reason, the title 'devotional' text is a helpful way of approaching Julian's writings. It expects her text to be not just a visionary or mystical curiosity, a passive receptacle of learning or a set of literary devices to dissect, but also a place of guidance and encounter.

I once gave a friend of mine a copy of *Revelations of Divine Love*. When I asked her later about how she liked Julian, she sighed and in a guilty manner informed me that a year on she was still only about halfway through. Apologising, I asked her if she had found the whole text too challenging. I have always remembered her reply: 'No,' she said. 'I think it's wonderful, but I can only read a couple of sentences a day. You cannot really read Julian; you can only pray it.' It seems to me that this is why a seemingly insignificant work in her day has become so popular in the 20th and 21st centuries: from her account of 16 revelations, Julian speaks to the spiritual life with which we all struggle in any age. The experience of entering her text leads us into that place where prayer is authentic. Without techniques or spiritual stages or visions of our own, her words simply do what she wanted them to do and what she felt was her mandate for writing – to point us to God.

At the foot of the cross with Julian

It is for this reason that reading Julian's text is such a prayerful experience, for through her words we are invited into a literary-constructed space that scaffolds a place of encounter for ourselves. Her words describe, explain, unfold, emote and deepen our relationship with God. It seems to me that this is why Julian is so often named by those who have read her as being one of the most influential of women in their lives.

This book, therefore, does not so much seek to replace Julian's own words and voice as unpack what she is saying. Part I explores how knowledge of her time and context can help illuminate our reading and allow her words to point the way and lead us to God, whereas each chapter of part II focuses on different aspects of her revelation of the cross: the crown of thorns, the face of Jesus, the blood, Jesus' thirst, the words of the thief, and Jesus' death. The biblical basis for Julian's vision is explored, along with the deeper meaning her vision reveals. This is set within the rich devotional context of the time in order to more fully understand the significance of Julian's interpretation of her visions and spiritual insight. Each chapter concludes with a guided reading exercise to enable you to enter the silence within Julian's words and with questions for personal devotion or discussion, as well as a verse of scripture for the journey.

Part I

– 1 –

ENTERING JULIAN'S WORLD

Julian lived in a world very different from our own. This is an obvious statement to make, but it is an important one to be aware of when approaching a text that was written in the 14th century. Sometimes it is tempting to extract Julian's writing from its context and culture and to read into it our own contemporary values and concerns, which are not there in Julian's work. That is not to say that there are not vestiges of the past still lingering in the present which enable us imaginatively to enter Julian's world. The medieval church of the past, despite all the whitewashing and removal of the centuries, can still be felt and heard today if you close your eyes and listen out for it.

When I worked at St Paul's Cathedral in London, each year, on the eve of Good Friday, something strange took place. Once all the grandeur and solemnity of the Maundy Thursday liturgy had come to an end, and the bejewelled chalices had been unceremoniously washed up and put away, the golden copes covered in white sheets and the doors banged shut, the work staff would come in. Any atmosphere of prayer and stillness was immediately shattered as they bantered in with jokes and flirtations for us, the vergers. Phil would slop down his bucket and begin to wash the floor to no avail, for soon it was streaked with lines as the staging was slowly wheeled over his work to be erected under the dome's enormity. Amid the clatter would come the calls of instruction: 'Where do you want this?' Ron would shout, as two enormous pieces of wood were dropped with an echo which resounded through the building and seemed to awaken the past and resurrect it in the present. Then the banging would start as the cross was gradually constructed and hoisted into place. The next day was Good Friday, and we were preparing for that solemnity, as others were across the country and the world, as one church, to realise the moment of Christ's death within the eternal now. But as I heard the clatter of construction and the banging of the nails, it was not so much Palestine that I saw in my mind's eye but the 14th-century world of clamour and clatter with its intense devotion to the cross.

Most of our medieval parishes have lost their rood screens now, but in the 14th century to enter a church was to enter a different world: a world peopled by the figures of scripture. Rising above these and looking down on all who entered this microcosm was the compassionate Christ, suspended upon his cross. From the rood screens that survive in Norfolk we have an idea, albeit a damaged one, of what they might have looked like. One of the most famous of these can be found in St Helen's Church, Ranworth, Norwich, where the 15th-century paintings are some of the best preserved in England (see Plate 1). The screen is wooden and separates the chancel, or altar end, from the body of the church. The lower part, or dado, is made up of wooden panels painted with saints, with central doors leading into the chancel. The paintings still show the twelve apostles, the three Marys, St Barbara, St Margaret, St Etheldreda, St Agnes and St John the Baptist (see Plate 2). Over this the tracery screen allows light into the nave and enables a clear view to the altar. This screen supports the loft, a place where the gospel would be read, candles lit and anthems sung. Raised high into the air would have been a wooden sculpture of Christ on the cross, flanked by Mary and John, now missing from St Helen's. This image would have dominated the space and captured any pilgrim's attention as they entered the church.

The dominance of the figures of the Passion within parish churches epitomised the importance of this moment in Christ's life within the devotional lives of ordinary people in the 14th century. During the medieval period, the representation of the Passion altered over time from being a statement of the triumph and lordship of Christ in the

Anglo-Saxon period to an image of the suffering human Jesus who hung upon this instrument of death solely out of love. Now Jesus was the man of pity, the man of sorrows, who evoked an emotional response from all who looked upon him. 'Is it nothing to you, all you who pass by?' – the words of Lamentations 1:12 rang out in accusation and awakening. Increasingly, images of the crucifixion scene dripped with blood as they sought to evoke strong feelings of pity and compassion from all who looked upon them.

This representation of the suffering Jesus was influenced and shaped by theological thinking as well as devotional practice and inspirational individuals. Archbishop Anselm in the eleventh century had convincingly argued his case against the pagans that in the face of Jesus Christ we see the image of the invisible God, who became man in order to pay the debt of sin. No one else but God himself could take on this role of sacrifice and restoration. The scene had been set to celebrate the human nature of Jesus. Then a century later the scholastic orator Peter Abelard argued that Jesus' death upon the cross was the highest demonstration of God's love for his people. His suffering brings forth compassion and pity from those who meditate on the cross, drawing them into a deeper relationship of love.

Alongside these theological understandings of the nature of the cross as sacrifice and love, the monastic world developed a reading of the gospels that involved greater personal participation and engagement. Anselm advocated meditation on the Passion to his sister as a means of evoking strong feelings of love and compassionate empathy with the suffering human Jesus. This meditative involvement was developed by the Franciscan Bonaventure and Cistercian Bernard of Clairvaux, both of whom understood the intense feelings that contemplation of the suffering Christ inspired in the soul as part of a spiritual process of compassion, contrition and longing for God. By this process our earthly desires were transformed into a spiritual love, which responded to and reflected the love of God, as demonstrated by Jesus on the cross. The devout were therefore encouraged to meditate freely on the story of the Passion in order to enhance their emotional engagement with the person of Jesus on the cross and enter the spiritual process of transformation. The word of scripture formed the base rock but, in a world where these words were invariably heard rather than read, the imagination was given free rein to embellish and bring alive the events of sacred history.

One of the most influential of the many meditations on the Passion was Nicholas Love's *The Mirror of the Blessed Life of Jesus Christ*, a late-medieval English translation of the very popular *Meditationes Vitae Christi*, which was wrongly attributed to Bonaventure. These meditations encapsulate the spiritual life of the late 14th century and were the only version of affective meditation that Archbishop Thomas Arundel would allow in his *Constitutions* of 1409, which sought to bring orthodoxy to the English church. Underlying them are the words of scripture as known through the Latin Vulgate, but the biblical events are supplemented by other apocryphal stories, in order to enable the reader to enter imaginatively into the historical narrative. In the introduction, Nicholas Love tells the reader how they are to approach this work:

> Wherefore you who truly desire to experience the fruit of this book, must with all your thought and all your intention make your soul present to those things that are written here about what our Lord said and did, and that as carefully, with such pleasure and constancy as if you heard them with your bodily ears or saw them with your own eyes.

Through meditation on the Passion, the past and the present were dissolved into one; the words on the page were no longer a record of the events of the past but a manifestation in the present moment of the eternal outpouring of Christ's love and a means of contemplative union with the beloved.

– 2 –

ENCOUNTER WITH A CRUCIFIX

It is within the culture of an intensely devotional and affective response to the love of Christ on the cross that Julian's visions begin to seem less strange and less suspect to our modern ears. In the late 14th century, it was part of the devotional norm, rather than a product of a delusional mind, to wish to imaginatively 'see' and 'feel' at first hand the dramatic events of the cross. Julian herself describes how, as a young girl, she had the same pious desires as anyone else of her age, to receive three gifts which echo the predominant devotional landscape of the day:

> The first was mind of his passion, the second was bodily sickness in my youth at 30 years of age, the third was to have of God's gift three wounds.

Julian tells us that she did have some feeling of his Passion within her prayer life but that she wanted more.

Just as the reader of *The Mirror of the Blessed Life of Jesus Christ* is directed to want to see the events and hear the words of scripture for themselves, so Julian desires to be:

> … with Mary Magdalen and all those others that were Christ's true lovers, and therefore I desired a bodily sight wherein I might have more knowledge of the bodily pains of our saviour and of the compassion of our lady and of all his true lovers who saw him in his pains, for I wanted to be one of them and suffer with them.

Julian is careful to tell us that she didn't want a vision of some kind; she wanted only to have a 'true mind' in the Passion of Jesus. She did not desire a special mystical favour; she desired to be given that devotional ability to be present in her mind's eye to the past events. In this way Julian is much like any other devout believer of her day. She sets the scene for the events which she is about to narrate; she is an ordinary person, no one special, just desiring the same imaginative engagement with the human person of Jesus on the cross as any other devotional person at that time. As she states, through this imaginative entering of the Passion narrative, Julian desires to feel for herself the same compassionate response to Christ's sufferings as was shown in those who were truly there. She wants to be like them, a true lover, in her response to the person of Christ on the cross and thereby receive the third gift: the wounds of contrition, compassion and longing for God.

At the heart of the medieval tradition of Passion meditations was this deeply personal and emotional encounter with the person of Jesus. To imaginatively stand at the foot of the cross was to enter a vulnerable space of emotional response to the suffering Jesus. Lyrics, meditative texts, art, music and architecture sought to heighten this engagement through use of emotive images and words. These often graphic and visceral expressions of the cross sought to make you weep at the suffering that Jesus bore, to prick your conscience at the awareness of the depth to which your own failings have contributed to that suffering and to elicit a profound attachment to the person who died on the cross for you.

While much of this medieval emotional headiness has gone from our Reformed churches, vestiges of it can still be experienced today. Enter any church or cathedral on Good Friday when John Sanders' setting of *The Reproaches* is being sung at the moment in the liturgy when you are invited to stand before the cross in a personal act of veneration, and you will feel something of our ancient medieval heritage. Dating from the ninth century, this set of antiphons and responses imagines Jesus' words of sorrow and accusation from the cross. Through a simple chant the many good deeds of God towards his people, and humanity's response, are objectively stated, only to conclude with the increasingly harrowing words of accusation: 'O my people, what have I done to you? How have I offended you? Answer me.' The experience is deeply moving, powerfully stark and, through Sanders' heart-rending harmonies, simply brings the worshipper to their knees in tears of compassion, contrition and longing for God, the same medieval spiritual attitude which opened the heart, absolved the penitent of sin and returned Christ's love and longing.

In May 1373 Julian understood her devotional request to stand in this place of spiritual and emotional encounter as being answered in the most dramatic and immediate way. In chapter 3 of *Revelations of Divine Love*, Julian outlines in detail the events that led up to her revelatory experience:

> And when I was thirty and a half years old, God sent me a bodily sickness in which I lay three days and three nights, and on the fourth night I took all my rites of holy church and believed not to live till day.

Julian was seriously ill, so ill that those around her believed she was going to die. As was normal at the time, the parish priest was called to give Julian the last rites. Then, as now, this liturgy of dying involved three elements: confession of one's sins along with the words of absolution from the priest, anointing with oil in preparation for death and the receiving of Communion or *viaticum*. Today it is often an intensely private occasion which bestows a great sense of peace and reassurance as the dying person is helped to lay to rest the things of the past and surrender to the loving arms of God. In Julian's day it was a more public event, as reflected in 15th-century depictions of the seven sacraments, such as that found in the stained-glass windows of St Michael's Church, Doddiscombsleigh, Devon (see Plate 3). Along with the family, the parish priest, altar boy and crucifer gathered to witness and be reassured that their loved one had made a 'good end' and was now ready to enter the next life through the mercy and forgiveness of the person of Jesus Christ, who died for sinners.

With a more acute notion that the acts of this life echoed throughout eternity and that there would be a reckoning, the need for the medieval sinner to clear their conscience of all those known and unknown sins in order to meet their maker was vital. Words of confession thought in the head were not enough; they had to be given actuality through speech for them to be made real. Therefore, aural confession to a priest at the time of death was not a pastoral preference but a mandatory necessity. In order to enable penitents to make as full and true a confession as possible, late 14th-century handbooks for clergy recommended that parish priests held an image of the cross before the dying person's eyes. Invariably this cross would have been a small handheld crucifix, much like one now in the Herbert Art Gallery and Museum in Coventry (see Plate 4). To look at an image of the person of Jesus on the cross was to be invited to enter that realm of imaginative and visual encounter with the suffering, crucified Jesus, which would evoke the deep emotional response of contrition, compassion and longing for God. The quality and depth of feeling sorry for one's sins was crucial for, by the end of the 14th century, the efficacy of the sacrament of confession was located not in the words of absolution, which the priest said, but in the contrition of the penitent. God looks upon the heart, and it is there that the sinner receives forgiveness. The priest completes that process by making real the spiritual words of forgiveness from Christ. The simple act of holding a crucifix before a dying person's eyes thereby becomes replete with significance as the state of a person's soul hangs in the balance.

After three days and nights of suffering, Julian received the last rites. She had been properly prepared for death and yet for a further two days and nights lingered in this liminal realm between living and dying. It was a time which most troubled those who thought and wrote about death and dying at the time. What if the soul in this in-between state committed a sin, however small – a bad thought or fear of death or, still worse, slipping into despair – when there was no more time to repent? Dying in a state of sinfulness preoccupied the medieval mind. Just as these priestly handbooks advised that the only sure salvation was for the dying person to keep their eyes fixed on the cross and throw themselves on Christ's mercy, so Julian's curate was called for once again:

> My curate was sent for so he could be at my ending, and by the time he came I had fixed my eyes and could not speak. He set the cross before my face and said, 'I have brought you the image of your maker and Saviour. Look thereupon and be comforted by it.'

At first Julian was reluctant to look at the cross; she had already received the last rites, and her eyes and soul were set heavenward to the place where she hoped, by the mercy of God, she would soon go. But, as a dutiful daughter of the church, she heeded her curate's words and lowered her gaze to 'set my eyes in the face of the crucifix'. Julian was invited once again to look at an image of the person of Jesus on the cross, but this time it was not in order to excite contrition. Instead, it was to reassure her of the compassion of Christ, who would hold her gaze in one of love and adoration that prevented any further sin.

It is from this encounter with the image of a crucifix that Julian's revelation flows. This is how Julian describes it:

> After this my sight began to fail, and it was all dark in the chamber around me, as if it were night, except for the image of the cross in which I beheld a common light, and I did not know how. All that was apart from the cross was ugly to me, as if it had been occupied with many fiends.

Julian's description is interesting for what it does not say as much as for what it does say. She is very precise in her description of what occurred on that evening in 1373 – there was no flash of lightning or parting of the clouds; rather, there was a gradual failure of her physical sight. Just as Julian's body was physically declining, now she describes a dying or, more precisely, a darkening of her physical eye. Everything was receding before her eyes, and all that was left was the physical representation of Jesus on the cross as depicted by the crucifix. This devotional object did not take on a supernatural glow or even a transcendent light, but, as her physical capacities failed, the cross came into clearer view. It was the only object she could see. It filled her vision, her world, as it became the only source of the normal, common or natural light.

– 3 –

JULIAN'S VISION OF THE PASSION

It was from the devotional representation of Jesus on the cross that Julian's subsequent visions of the Passion flow. Even as she watched the crucifix take on this 'common light', Julian was reminded of her pious childhood wishes, which over the years she had come to forget, as now they began to make sense:

> Suddenly it came to my mind that I should desire the second wound, by the Lord's gracious gift, and that my body might be filled with the mind and feeling of his blessed Passion; for I wanted his pains to be my pains with compassion and afterwards longing for God. But in this wish I never desired a physical sight or showing from God, only compassion, as a natural soul would want for our Lord Jesus, who for love became a mortal man and therefore I desired to suffer with him.

By making this connection between her past devotional wishes and the unfolding of her revelation, Julian is not only associating her visionary experience with the meditative practices of the day, but also rooting her very personal revelation within the devotional framework of the Passion meditation. It was from the intense engagement with the biblical narrative of the cross, as expressed in the devotional object of the crucifix, that Julian's imaginative visions sprung.

Julian, like anyone of her day, would have known the story of the Passion extremely well, though it is unlikely that she would have read the scriptures first-hand, as we do today. English Wycliffite Bibles were in circulation at this time but, as a good daughter of the church, Julian probably would not have owned or even wanted to own such a subversive book, for which she could have been condemned for heresy if she had possessed one. Instead, the late 14th century was an aural-centred world, where the text of scripture was heard read aloud in church, seen enacted in plays and imaginatively entered into through Passion meditations. Via these different media Julian would have engaged differently with scripture than we do today. As we have seen, she would have been encouraged to 'own' and embellish the narrative until it became real and living to her, rather than it being a historical document of sacred text. Hence the Passion image or text is but the beginning from which Julian's revelations emerge. The showing that develops seeks not to supplant scripture but to ruminate on it until there is a deeper knowledge of and engagement with Christ. Hence, at their core, her showings are centred on the gospel narrative of the cross:

- First revelation – crowning of thorns (Mark 15:17; Matthew 27:29; John 19:2)
- Second revelation – Christ on the cross (Mark 15:33–34; Matthew 27:45–46)
- Fourth revelation – mocking and scourging (Mark 15:19; Matthew 27:30; John 19:1; Luke 22:63)
- Eighth revelation – the thirst and death of Christ (Mark 15:37; Matthew 27:50; Luke 23:46; John 19:28–30 – 'I thirst')
- Ninth revelation – Christ's words to the thief, 'Today you will be with me in Paradise' (Luke 23:43)
- Tenth revelation – the piercing of Christ's side with a lance (John 19:32–37)
- Eleventh revelation – Mary at the foot of the cross (Matthew 27:56; John 19:25)

Each of these seven showings are rooted in the scriptural events of Jesus' Passion, but very quickly pass from the word on a page to personal encounter with the Word through revelation. In the first five of these revelations, it is the suffering human Jesus who we are brought before as they linger on the pain of the Passion and the slow process of his dying, whereas with the tenth revelation the tone changes markedly and the scriptural basis to the revelations become a springboard to contemplate salvation through the cross and our personal relationship with Christ as a result. In this book, however, we linger at the foot of the cross and stay with Christ in his suffering and death, focusing solely on the first five Passion showings.

Julian's revelations differ markedly from other visions of the time. Just up the road from Julian, at King's Lynn, Margery Kempe was disclosing her visionary experiences to anyone who would listen. Much like the later meditations of Ignatius Loyola, Margery imaginatively inhabited the world of the biblical narrative and took an active role within them. In contrast to Margery, Julian's visions are somewhat different. While scripture is at the core of Julian's revelation – the starting point and focus – it is the spark from which Julian enters into a deeper knowledge and encounter with the person of Christ as the events of the Passion unfold before her eyes. Not surprisingly, Julian's revelations are often seen as a product of *lectio divina* on the Passion, the Benedictine process of sacred reading, whereby a person would study scripture, focusing on the letter of the word, then meditating on its sense, followed by prayer, or loving conversation with God, and finally into the silence of contemplation.

In chapter 9 of *Revelations of Divine Love*, Julian describes the different ways in which she was shown her revelation, which resonates with Augustinian teaching on the three modes of seeing:

> And all this was shown in three parts: that is to say, by bodily sight and by words formed in my understanding and by spiritual sight. But the spiritual sight I cannot nor may not show as clearly nor as fully as I would wish.

There is a sense in which these three forms of showing are progressive: one moves from physical sight to spiritual and finally intellectual sight. But a feature of Julian's revelatory account that is common to other female mystics of her day is that the three forms of visionary showing are invariably collapsed into one. In her writings Julian thereby gives us what she 'observed' with her physical sight, what she 'saw' in her imagination and finally what she experienced through her intellectual vision. But, like the experience itself, these three elements are interwoven within her text so tightly that the highly graphic and visual accounts of what she saw with her own eyes cannot be easily dissociated from her rational verbalisation of what she saw or spiritual understanding of them. For Julian, it is clear that the combination of all three constitutes her divine revelation. God reveals himself through the interface between these different modes of disclosure: scripture, bodily experiences, devotional practice, religious objects, meditation, language, interpretation, encounter and illumination. In Julian's *Revelations of Divine Love* you will therefore find not a simple description of a visionary experience which Julian then comments upon, but rather a rich, if heady, mix of nigh on 20 years of inner thought, reflection and prayer on an experience that is couched in the language and images of the late 14th-century devotional culture, all of which together reveals something new and stunning about the love of God who died on the cross.

Part II

*

The first revelation

– 4 –

THE CROWN OF THORNS

This chapter considers the crowning of Jesus and links it in with suffering and humiliation. Differentiating between humiliation and humility, the chapter moves to contemplate the image for Julian as an icon of the loving humility of God.

As Julian lay in bed, intently gazing on the wooden crucifix that her priest held before her eyes, as if out of nowhere it transformed into a visionary encounter with a moment in the Passion narrative: the crowning of Jesus with a coronet of thorns.

> In this suddenly I saw the red blood trickling down from under the garland, hot and freshly and right plenteously, as if it was the time of his Passion when the garland of thorns was pressed on to his blessed head, right so both God and man, the same that suffered for me. I conceived truly and mightily that it was himself who showed it without any intermediary.
>
> *Revelations of Divine Love*, ch. 4

This is the first of 16 revelations that were given to Julian across a three-day period. In fact, she tells us very little of what she actually saw. There is barely a line to describe the visionary content of her revelation, yet the words she uses are so evocative and compact that we are given all the imaginary tools we need to construct our own mental image of what she saw. Like the alarm call of Advent, Julian's words wake us up to something new and startling. To begin with it is uncertain whether Julian sees the wooden cross actually bleeding. Such fantastical events were not uncommon in the medieval period, but soon it becomes clear that the crucifix is only the physical, devotional trigger point for the unfolding of a visual scene which has its roots in the biblical narrative of the Passion.

Scriptural beginnings

The scriptural basis to Julian's vision is an equally brief, albeit significant, moment in the Passion narrative. All the gospel writers record the mocking and humiliation which Jesus suffered at the hands of his captors in the hours before his crucifixion. Yet it is Mark, Matthew and John who specifically attribute this humiliating treatment of Jesus to the Roman soldiers, who sought to mock Jesus' given title of King of the Jews. This was not an identity Jesus had given to himself; rather, it was placed upon him by others, especially by the Roman governor Pilate, who then had it inscribed above Jesus' cross. Perhaps it was also a title given to him more generally by those who had hoped Jesus was a kind of military leader who would overthrow the Roman empire and usher in the new kingdom of the Lord, as prophesied of old. By the time of his crucifixion it had become one of ridicule and jest.

The gospel writers recount a series of actions which were designed to dehumanise Jesus and strip away his sense of identity and worth. The first was the removal of all Jesus' clothes until he stands silently before the soldiers naked. The brevity of the account in Matthew 27:28 permits us to pass over this fact quickly, but if we allow our imaginations to give life to these simple words, then it is a place of naked humiliation that is hard to inhabit. Second, Jesus was forced to take on a false identity as he is wrapped in a robe of scarlet, the emblem of kingship, which visually not only misrepresents but also undermines all that Jesus was and came to do. It is as if he stands on the pinnacle of the desert temple once again and the devil not only shows him all the nations of the earth but they also laugh at him. Central to this performance of denigration was Jesus' mock crowning by the soldiers. Three of the gospel accounts tell of how they twisted some thorns into the shape of a crown and placed it on Jesus' head. This crown was an object meant to cause great pain, both physically and psychologically.

It was this moment of painful humiliation that Julian saw in her first revelation as she lay on her bed seriously ill and looking at a wooden crucifix. Her vision arises from an object of devotion that captures the biblical narrative of the Passion. However, what Julian saw, and how she describes her vision, is very different from the scriptural moment of the crowning of Christ with thorns. From her words we do not get the sense that Julian imaginatively recreated the scene of the crowning of thorns in her mind's eye, as one would do in a meditation. Neither was she wondrously transported to the historical moment in order to participate in it, like other visionaries describe. She did not stand alongside the soldiers as they bound the thorns together and placed it on Jesus' head in order for her to weep in compassion at the humiliation of our Lord. Nor did the wooden crucifix miraculously seem to bleed before her eyes, an impression perhaps brought on through her extreme illness. Instead, Julian was given a revelation which sprang from a moment in the Passion narrative. Scripture is the beginning point and also the departure point for what she saw.

Julian's account of her revelation grows and develops, sometimes focusing on one image, at other times ranging into another image altogether, and amid these showings, intertwined even, is Julian's interpretation and understanding of it. It is as if Julian's revelation is dependent on her interpretation and understanding; the sight does not stand alone without Julian's words, so fragile is it until Julian's narrative holds it for us to explore. It is these words we now look at.

A garland of joy

When we turn to Julian's description of her first revelation, it is not the sense of the humiliation of Jesus by the soldiers at the crowning of thorns that is expressed, but rather the image of a garland. The word leaps out from the page of Julian's text. In the Greek New Testament, the gospel writers use the word *stephanos*, which referred to the crown of exaltation given to victors of the games and to victorious generals for their glorious achievements in war, in addition to the more usual sense of a kingly adornment and symbol of power and authority. However, this was not the sense of the word Julian would have known. In the Latin Vulgate, the Greek term *stephanos* was translated by Jerome as *coronam de spinis*, which has its roots in another Greek term, *korone*, meaning a garland or a wreath. It was this meaning of the crown that was prevalent during the medieval period. Moreover, for a world which was still inhabited by tokens of the Passion, it was the word 'garland' that best expressed the wreath of twisted reeds that was one of the central relics of the medieval church. People understood the crown of thorns as a garland, because they had seen it with their own eyes.

On the first Friday of the month and every Friday in Lent a remarkable act of devotion has taken place in Notre Dame in Paris until the recent tragic fire there. Preceded by cross, acolytes, priests and members of religious orders, and surrounded by billowing clouds of incense, the crown of thorns is brought into the cathedral to be venerated by the faithful. Housed in a circlet of crystal and gold, this most holy of relics has been reduced to a simple bundle of reeds, the thorns having been distributed over the centuries, but its spiritual power is in no way diminished for those pilgrims who flock from around the world to see it, or even kiss it, on Good Friday. One of those precious thorns that King Louis IX and his descendants sent as gifts across Europe can be found in its 14th-century reliquary in the British Museum today (see Plate 5). There is no incense, no ritual or priest, but I wonder if those who peer through the glass and gaze at the single spike surrounded by golden images of Christ in glory are moved by a similar sense of awe and curiosity as pilgrims to Notre Dame have been.

It is this same sense of a garland that we find in the devotional writing of the time. For example, in *The Privity of the Passion*, an English version of the early 14th-century *Meditationes Vitae Christi* by Johannes de Caulibus, a detailed, affective devotional text, the moment of the crowning with thorns is described in these terms: 'They take a garland of sharp thorns instead of a crown and thrust it on his head.' In this graphic description, which epitomises the way in which the crown of thorns was viewed within medieval devotional culture, the garland of sharp thorns is contrasted with the image of a victorious crown. The physical pain it causes is emphasised as well as the way it was used to humiliate Jesus as a mock crown. This meaning of the word 'garland' is also brought out in the 15th-century carol, where Christ is addressed with the words, 'How shalt thou sufferin the scharp garland of thorns?'

Many texts and songs which use the word 'garland' were written specifically to enable the reader actively to engage and meditate on the events of the Passion. The reader was invited to spend time looking at and thinking on the significance of the thorns. This focused devotional engagement with one specific event of the Passion was further enhanced and reinforced by the new liturgical feasts that had been added to the calendar, as well as devotion to relics of the holy thorns. Along with the remembrance of the Passion on Good Friday there were further occasions to express devotion to the sufferings of Jesus through the feasts of the five wounds, the crown of thorns and the name of Jesus. These tokens of the Passion became stylised into emblems, a devotional shorthand which focused on the specific events of the cross. The crown of thorns was included among them and can be found on the frame of the Despenser Retable in Norwich Cathedral, which dates from Julian's day (see Plate 6). The central panels of the retable depict scenes from the Passion narrative which visually seek to draw the viewer into an affective meditation on the events (see Plate 7). Their large eyes, flowing blood and strange contorted gestures exhort us to linger and look until the events of the Passion narrative become real and present to us and we imaginatively see them for ourselves in our mind's eye.

Julian's use of the word 'garland', therefore, did not spring from a vacuum. As a devout young woman she would have looked at, prayed with and meditated on the instruments of the cross. Her revelation is a distillation of that devotional heritage in which she stood. Yet her contribution to this culture is to move us, her reader, at light speed from a recognition that the crown of thorns is an instrument of humiliation and pain to an experience of joy and celebration, such as she felt at the time of her revelation.

It is this joyful association of the word 'garland' that we find more often in the Old Testament and which resonates for us today with the image of joy and festivity. In the book of Proverbs, the author exhorts his child to seek wisdom, for if he does, 'she [Wisdom] will place on your head a fair garland [*corona*]' (Proverbs 4:9). Here a garland is a thing of honour and beauty which is to be prized and sought. It is an adornment rather than a symbol of power or victory. For the author of Proverbs, it is Wisdom who bestows such a crown. When we hear or read the word 'garland', it is invariably this image of summer and joy that is called to mind, for garlands are more often associated with flowers than they are with thorns. So we find garlands of roses adorning church porches to welcome a bride on her wedding day and children linking daisies together to crown their parents with a garland of flowers. This understanding of the word 'garland' is in complete contradiction to the suffering and humiliating *stephanos* of thorns placed on Jesus' head, a fact not lost on Julian, who brings the two conflicting images together through her use of the word 'garland' rather than 'crown', a symbol of horror and humiliation with the garland of wisdom and joy.

In her showing, Julian saw beyond and through the historical and devotional depiction of the gospels and began to comprehend not the sense of the letter of the scripture but rather its meaning. The key to this can be found in another biblical reference to the garland. In Isaiah 61:3 one of the defining features of the one who brings good news is that they give to those who are oppressed, broken-hearted and captive 'a garland [*coronam*] instead of ashes'. It is this very passage which Jesus stands up and reads in the synagogue in Nazareth, thereby setting out the mandate for his ministry:

> The Spirit of the Lord is upon me, because he has anointed me to bring good news to the poor. He has sent me to proclaim release to the captives and recovery of sight to the blind, to let the oppressed go free, to proclaim the year of the Lord's favour.
> LUKE 4:18–19

Jesus is identified as the one who will give us a garland instead of ashes.

In contemplating the moment of Jesus' crowning of thorns, Julian's eyes focused not just on the thorns, for she was given a sight – or should I say an insight – into what this crown meant in relation to the person who was being crowned. For Jesus this was an emblem of humiliation and suffering, but, at the same time, he transformed this crown into a garland of joy. It is as if Julian has looked on the crown of thorns in all its mocking and humiliation long enough to come to see what was going on and that, through Jesus wearing this crown, it was for him, and now for us, a garland of wisdom, beauty and reconciliation. In the rest of chapter 4, Julian marvels at this insight that the person we see crowned with thorns at his Passion was 'right so both God and man'. This statement concerning the nature of Christ opens up a further revelation for Julian, as she discovers a new way of seeing the Passion, taking us with her. She writes:

> And in the same showing, suddenly the Trinity fulfilled the heart most of joy. And so I understood it shall be in heaven without end to all that shall come there. For the Trinity is God, God is the Trinity; the Trinity is our maker and keeper; the Trinity is our everlasting lover, everlasting joy and bliss, by our Lord Jesus Christ. And this was shown in the first and in all; for where Jesus appears the blessed Trinity is understood, as to my sight. And I said, 'Benedicte domine!'

Julian could not contain herself, and she burst out in words of praise. She has indeed been given a garland of joy instead of ashes. Her words capture this eureka moment for us; her revelation has shown that the person who suffered on the cross like an ordinary criminal was not alone. There is a solidarity in his suffering with all who are equally humiliated and violently tortured. He shares the pain of all those who cry out, 'Why have you forsaken me?' Yet within this cruel crown of thorns is also the garland of wisdom, for Julian perceives that while it is the human Jesus who suffers, the whole blessed Trinity is present. Her revelation does not linger on an image of mutilation and torture, delighting in a morbid sense of curiosity for the macabre and sensational suffering of the cross. Instead, she bids us look, meditate and see the wisdom of God on the cross. This realisation and understanding transformed Julian's ashes into joy, as she was suddenly overwhelmed by the realisation of what God has done in Christ. Her revelation has brought her from a place of observing humiliation, which was the bedrock of medieval devotion, to an expression of humility.

Going deeper

Spend a few moments allowing the words of the chapter to settle in your mind.

Before you read Julian's words again, ask God to speak to you through them. What word or insight does he have for you today?

As you slowly reread Julian's words, allow your imagination to picture what she is saying, and be open to where your thoughts and ideas may take you.

> In this suddenly I saw the red blood trickling down from under the garland, hot and freshly and right plenteously, as if it was the time of his Passion when the garland of thorns was pressed on to his blessed head, right so both God and man, the same that suffered for me. I conceived truly and mightily that it was himself who showed it without any intermediary.

Reflect for a moment on where your thoughts were led. What spoke to you and why?

Instead of trying to silence your inner thoughts and feelings, let them float by like the flowing water of a stream and allow your attention to go deeper into silence for as little or as long as you wish.

What will you take away with you from this time of meditation?

Questions to ponder or discuss

- How did this passage make you feel?
- What does the cross mean for you?
- What difference does Christ's suffering make to times when you have suffered?
- What difference does Christ's suffering make to the suffering of others?
- What joy could you bring to a sorrowful situation this week?

Words for the journey

> For the message about the cross is foolishness to those who are perishing, but to us who are being saved it is the power of God.
> 1 CORINTHIANS 1:18

– 5 –

GOD IS THE TRINITY

Continuing her meditation on the vision of the crowning of thorns, Julian marvels at the 'homely' loving of the Trinity and the presence of the three persons with Christ on the cross. This chapter explores our response to the humility of God on the cross as one of self-emptying.

Visually, the presence of the whole Trinity at the cross was represented during the 14th century by the image of the Throne of Grace, in which God the Father, seated on his throne, holds the cross of Christ. The Holy Spirit hovers above, as seen in the mid-13th-century Carrow Psalter (see Plate 8), named for the convent at Carrow, which was situated close to Julian's cell.

This representation, like all attempts at depicting the Trinity, falls short because of one of two errors: either to emphasise the different persons to the detriment of their unity or to focus on their unified substance and neglect to give proper weight to the differentiated persons. The Throne of Grace in the Carrow Psalter falls into the former category, because it depicts the distinct persons of the Trinity that are only clearly unified by the letter 'O', the circle of eternity. Julian, however, sidesteps such theological traps. She does not seek to describe a theological mystery or a linguistic paradox. Instead, she captures, through her words, a revelatory moment – an experience of when the scales fell from her eyes, when the proverbial light in the room was switched on:

> And in the same showing suddenly the Trinity fulfilled the heart most of joy. And so I understood it shall be in heaven without end to all that shall come there.

Her text describes and captures her exuberant outpouring of praise to the Trinity that arose from a moment of insight, which sets the tone for the rest of the chapter.

It is interesting that this praise to the Trinity is not found in the shorter version of Julian's writings. It is only later, as she has had time to unpack her experience and consider it in relation to her whole revelation, that she could return to add this encomium of the presence of God:

> For the Trinity is God, God is the Trinity; the Trinity is our maker and keeper; the Trinity is our everlasting lover, everlasting joy and bliss, by our Lord Jesus Christ.

Through her words she sought to hold the persons of the Trinity in their substance in a way that the Throne of Grace was never able to do. While Julian's words capture that interweaving unity of the Trinity, it is her exuberance which draws us as a reader into her experience as she moves from first-person singular, 'I saw', to third-person possessive pronoun, 'our everlasting lover... our Lord Jesus Christ'. Drawing us into this same sense of homeliness with the Trinity as she herself experienced, she writes:

> This I said, for reverence in my meaning, with a mighty voice; and full greatly was I astounded with wonder and marvel that he who is so reverend and dreadful would be so homely with a sinful creature living in wretched flesh.

On one level Julian is speaking about herself, but following her encomium this statement is more encompassing. We too are the sinful creatures who, like her, live in this wretched flesh, but as she has witnessed in her revelation, so too for us, the garland of thorns is a symbol of joy and the presence of the Trinity in a uniquely homely and familiar way.

The *homlyhede* of God

The Middle English word *homlyhede* has been translated in various different ways, from 'home-like' to 'familiar' or 'informal'. In each case there is the same social relationship. For this reason, it is often contrasted with the more courtly language of 'courtesy', which Julian often uses to describe our relationship with God. It is true that the word 'homely' can be understood as having a ring of familiarity and domestic intimacy, but the term was also used to describe a spiritual, even mystical, state in which the soul is united with God, echoing perhaps Paul's words in Galatians, 'It is no longer I who live, but it is Christ who lives in me' (Galatians 2:20).

Contemporaneous 14th-century devotional writers also express this understanding of the word 'homely'. Walter Hilton writes of being 'transformed with God, and that is when his soul is so oned [united] with Christ, and right homely with him'. The *Cloud* author observes that some would-be contemplatives are 'so homely with God in this grace of contemplacion', in the sense of being over-familiar. This could easily be a statement of abuse, revealing some of the pitfalls of the possessive nature of some would-be contemplatives. Julian may well have known some of these connotations, yet she uses and develops the word in her own unique way. This is the first of several times that Julian uses 'homely', but each time its meaning shifts slightly as she moulds it in her hands to express a deepening awareness of the nature of our relationship with God.

It is in chapter 5 that Julian begins to unpack the meaning of the state of *homlyhede*, the insight into our intimate relationship with God that she gained from her first revelation of the crowning of thorns. In so doing, she takes us, the reader, on a journey to realisation and encounter. The chapter opens with Julian locating us within her visionary world. Up to this moment we have been focusing on her bodily sight of one of the events of the Passion, the crowning of thorns; now we purposefully move to a ghostly or spiritual sight, which takes us to the realm of understanding and image as Julian sees by divine illumination alone. The signifiers of the devotional world are now at rest, and Julian receives insight into the homely loving of God. She expresses this through an image of clothing:

> He is our clothing that for love wraps around us, embraces us and all encloses us for tender love that he may never leave us, being to us everything that is good, as to my understanding.

On one level we are presented with a purely domestic image, to show us the extent to which God is part of our everyday lives. He is not like a grand liturgical cope to be worn as at a ceremonial occasion but like our ordinary clothes that we wear daily to keep us warm and covered. There is even the sense of this love swaddling us like a baby. One scholar has interpreted the image within the context of Julian's deathbed situation and likened the cloth to a shroud that is wrapped around a body at death.

On another level the word 'homely' also holds the theological connotations of being humble. In the previous chapter, we find Julian using it in exactly these terms as she marvels at the humility of God who has become so homely with a sinful creature, thereby echoing Paul's letter to the Philippians:

> Let the same mind be in you as was in Christ Jesus, who, though he was in the form of God, did not regard equality with God as something to be exploited, but emptied himself, taking the form of a slave, being born in human likeness. And being found in human form, he humbled himself and became obedient to the point of death – even death on a cross.
>
> PHILIPPIANS 2:5–8

Julian expresses the humility of Christ on the cross in terms of a domestic image of clothing to convey the extent to which God's love humbly enters everyday human life, in order to enclose us and be everything that is good for us. So the chapter opens with an image of the humility of God but also our need of him.

The littleness of creation

From being the centre of attention and the subject of God's love, the perspective suddenly shifts, and we are shown our comparative insignificance; we are shown the extent of our need for God:

> Also in this he showed a little thing, the quantity of a hazelnut in the palm of my hand; and it was as round as a ball.

We have moved rapidly from a domestic image of the homely love of God to this sight of something very small, which Julian likens to the size of a hazelnut. However, she doesn't know what it is. The answer she is given is that it is everything that is made, this world, the universe; all that is comprehended by us is tiny, insignificant, as small as a hazelnut:

> I marvelled how it might exist, for methought it might suddenly have fallen to nought for its littleness. And I was answered in my understanding: it exists and ever shall, because God loves it, and so all things have their being through the love of God.

We have moved with some sense of vertigo from seeing ourselves at the centre of this world to suddenly seeing with God's eyes and realising that, in relationship to him, we are tiny. It is the same dichotomy that can be found in Psalm 8:

> When I look at your heavens, the work of your fingers, the moon and the stars that you have established; what are human beings that you are mindful of them, mortals that you care for them?
> PSALM 8:3–4

It is interesting that Julian is not so much fazed by this revelation, not reduced or overwhelmed by the knowledge of her insignificance. Instead, she just marvels that it is there at all and hasn't collapsed into nothingness because of its littleness. She hasn't really asked a question, but her marvelling results in an answer, and the answer expresses the notion that everything has its being because it is held in God's hand. This same notion is expressed in the 13th-century retable at Westminster Abbey, which depicts Jesus holding the globe in his hand (see Plate 9). The world is sustained because God loves it and because his love is what gives it its being.

Maker, keeper, lover

Julian then moves into a theological explanation of the initial clothing image of the homely love of God and reveals the extent to which that love not only created but also sustains everything that is made, including us. Today, some people get worked up about the doctrine of the Trinity and how difficult it is to explain, so that the Christian faith becomes largely focused on the person of Jesus and following him. But Julian has none of those qualms and feels no need to rationalise mystery. Instead, she has a robust engagement with the notion of the Trinity, and so here she uses trinitarian language to reveal the extent to which God is intimately involved in creating and sustaining all that is made. Yet she is fully aware of that ultimate mystery:

> But what is to me truly the maker, the keeper, and the lover
> I cannot tell.

In other words, 'I don't have a clue.' Through her writing, Julian has moved us from a place where we were the centre of all God's homely loving to the realisation that we know nothing, to the dependency of our littleness. She shows us, through her revelation, what we really are and the extent to which we are totally reliant on God.

Self-emptying

We come now to the heart of the chapter, as Julian turns to our relationship with God. From starting with the humility of God, the self-emptying of Christ on the cross, Julian now addresses the need for our own self-emptying, so that we can humbly recognise that we will only have rest and peace once we are fully aware of our reliance on and our need of God. We are humbly to fasten ourselves like a belt on to him, just as he wrapped and enclosed us in his garments of homely love. Julian uses the language of 'noughting' to describe this:

> For, till I am substantially one with him, I may never have full rest nor true bliss; that is to say, that I be so fastened to him that there is right nothing that is made between my God and me. It needs us to have knowledge of the littleness of creatures and to nought everything that is made for to love and have God that is unmade.

As some scholars have said, in this language of 'noughting' Julian takes us to the very edge of the apophatic, where words and images are negated in order to come to the darkness beyond knowing, where God can only be encountered through love. Julian is referring to a tradition of spiritual and contemplative learning that was flowering at that time, but she is also coming dangerously close to some of the more heretical thoughts of the movement known as Free Spiritism, epitomised in the writings of Marguerite Porete, in which the soul is annihilated or subsumed into the nature of God. Julian never goes that far, because, unlike Porete, she doesn't fully dispense with the devotional life of the church but instead embeds this process of 'noughting' or humble self-emptying within the doctrinal and sacramental life of the church, especially the process of confession.

We can see this in the language Julian uses to describe how a soul is to nought itself. She writes:

> It is full great pleasance to him that a sily [innocent] soul come to him nakedly and plainly and homely. For this is the natural yearnings of the soul by the touching of the Holy Ghost.

Julian is talking about the way in which the Holy Spirit inspires the process by which the soul is to empty itself, but the language she uses to describe this contemplative act of noughting is in fact penitential. In the 14th-century church, there were 16 so-called marks that were required to make a confession true and full. Three of these were that the penitent's confession must be 'naked', 'plain' and 'humbly' made. These marks were not only set out in the rule for anchoresses, the *Ancrene Wisse*, which Julian probably knew, but were standard to penitential practice in the late 14th century. Julian specifically describes the stirrings of contrition in terms of 'the touching of the Holy Ghost'. This penitential language would not have been lost on the intended 14th-century devotional reader of her text. Therefore, the process of self-emptying, in order to be substantially united and fully reliant on God, is located by Julian within the very processes of the church that sought to enable the contrite soul to see itself in relation to God and its need of him. Julian has brought us to the edge of the apophatic, but she has also affirmed the confessional disciplines of the church as the means for ensuring that there is 'right nothing' between our God and us.

As if to realise this, Julian's words shift into the language of prayer. We are not just drawn by her into a contemplative silence, or even a mystical experience, but are encouraged to speak these words for ourselves, which give voice to that humble recognition by the soul that all it needs is God and anything less falls short:

> God of thy goodness give me thyself; for thou art enough to me and I may nothing ask that is less that may be full worship to thee. And if I ask anything that is less, ever am I in need, but only in thee I have all.

So Julian's words become ours, and her text brings us to that forum of encounter and prayer.

Cleaving to his goodness

It is from this experience of a spontaneous outpouring of a need for God in recognition of the littleness of our being that Julian understands the quintessential nature of prayer as being a cleaving to God's goodness. Behind this statement on prayer, Julian inverts our normal understanding of what it means to pray.

Often we see prayer as essentially a human activity. We say our prayers and participate in liturgy. We use techniques, words and spiritual books to help us develop our prayer life. Liturgical acts of worship, meditation, contemplation or saying an office are scaffolding to help our prayer time. Our time of silence may have been barely free of thoughts, but at least we turned up and tried to bombard the cloud of unknowing, which the *Cloud* author describes as existing between ourselves and God with arrows of love and desire.

Likewise, in Julian's time prayer was principally about what you did. The services were in Latin, but this did not discount your participation; even if the office was said on your behalf by a priest, your bodily presence was still required. The saying of rote prayers was the norm. It was a time of the 'bidding of beads', as William Langland described prayer. If Julian did indeed follow the suggested office set out by the *Ancrene Wisse*, there would barely have been a moment when she was not vocalising a *Pater noster*, *Credo* or *Gloria*. The medieval period was full of the voicing of words to Christ where the focus was on the one who prayed.

However, in chapter 6 of *Revelations of Divine Love*, Julian shifts the focus somewhat and follows Paul's understanding that prayer is essentially not something we do but is something which God does within and through us, as set out in his letter to the Romans:

> Likewise the Spirit helps us in our weakness; for we do not know how to pray as we ought, but that very Spirit intercedes with sighs too deep for words. And God, who searches the heart, knows what is the mind of the Spirit, because the Spirit intercedes for the saints according to the will of God.
>
> ROMANS 8:26–27

As I sit in my study and ponder all the books on prayer that I have accumulated over the years, I can't help thinking that, however worthy and good they are, invariably I have used them as a replacement for actually praying. It's all too easy to enjoy reading about prayer, rather than actually doing it. In her book on prayer, the art historian and solitary Sister Wendy Beckett wrote that prayer is essentially simple: we just have to want to pray. But the hard thing comes next: if we want to pray, then we have to let God pray in us. We have to recognise our littleness and hand the controls over to him. While we are still structuring our prayer practices around what we like or what we think works, we are still in control; prayer is still about us and can border on self-improvement. Whereas, through her writing, Julian brings her reader to that attitude of humble recognition of our need of God, which enables God to begin to pray in and through us.

Julian does not, however, then discard the prayer practices of her time. She does not stipulate a mystical trance in glorious self-isolation and blessed peace; rather, she redefines the role of the everyday devotional homage to the many feasts which had been brought in to commemorate Christ's Passion, including the precious blood and crown of thorns. Julian describes these, along with devotion to Mary and the saints, as the means or conduits of God's goodness:

> For God of his goodness has ordained means to help us, which are fair and many, of which the chief and principal means is the blessed nature that he took from the maiden, to our redemption and to endless salvation. Wherefore it pleases him

> that we seek him and worship by means, understanding and knowing that he is the goodness of all, for the goodness of God is the highest prayer and it comes down to the lowest part of our need.

In an image that echoes the descent of the Holy Spirit to Mary at the visitation, God's goodness permeates down through Christ's humanity into the lowest depths of our need:

> For as the body is clad in the cloth, and the flesh in the skin, and the bones in the flesh, and the heart in the trunk of the body, so are we, soul and body, clad in the goodness of God and enclosed; yea, and more homely, for all these may waste and wear away, but the goodness of God is ever whole and more near to us without any likeness; for truly our lover desires that our soul cleave to him with all the might and that we be evermore cleaving to his goodness.

Julian returns once more to the initial image of the homeliness of God, whose love enfolds and encloses us in himself, but she now reveals in very visceral, incarnational terms how completely we are reliant on Christ, both bodily and spiritually, for his goodness. And it is God's will that we simply cleave to him, knowing how much we are loved and sustained, held and enclosed by him. For then God's goodness and love is reciprocated and made complete in our love and longing for him.

For Julian, the model and icon of this relationship of love is revealed in the person of Mary. She is the pattern of the one who prays:

> That is to mean the high wisdom and truth she had in beholding her maker so great, so high, so mighty and so good. This greatness and this nobleness of the beholding of God fulfilled her with reverend dread, and with this she saw herself so little and so low, so simple and so poor, in respect of her Lord God, that this reverand dread filled her with meekness. And thus, on

> this ground, she was filled with grace and all manner of virtues and surpassed all creatures.

Julian describes the attitude as one of reverent dread, awe at the greatness of God and humble recognition of herself as so little, so low, so poor and so simple, the same attitude of 'noughting' that we found in chapter 5. For Julian, Mary is not just an intercessor, but the model of the relationship that God yearns to have with all his creatures. It is the attitude of prayer that Julian invites us to articulate for ourselves through her very words.

Spend some time with the words of Julian's prayer.

> God of thy goodness give me thyself; for thou art enough to me, and I may nothing ask that is less that may be full worship to thee. And if I ask anything that is less, ever am I in need, but only in thee I have all.

Reflect on a time when God felt very close to you, enfolding you in his love. What was it that enabled you to feel close to God?

Reflect on a time when God felt distant. What was it that prevented you from knowing and feeling God's presence?

What are the needs and secret longings of your heart that you would like to lay before Jesus?

Allowing your inner thoughts and feelings to settle like ripples on a pond, enter the deeper place of silence and peace.

What will you take away with you from this time of meditation?

Questions to ponder or discuss

- How do you envisage and understand God as Trinity?
- What does humility mean for you?
- What do you find hard in prayer and in what ways could you overcome it?
- To whom could you embody the enfolding love of Christ?
- What could you do this week to nurture and sustain our fragile world?

Words for the journey

> I have been crucified with Christ; and it is no longer I who live, but it is Christ who lives in me.
>
> GALATIANS 2:19–20

– 6 –

GREAT DROPLETS OF BLOOD

In the previous reflection, on the vision of the crowning of thorns, Julian focuses on the great droplets of blood that run from Christ's garland. Drawing on the medieval language and imagery of the precious nature of Jesus' blood, this chapter highlights the manner in which Julian's vision and language express the overflowing gift of salvation in everyday life.

In all the time that he showed this that I have said now in ghostly sight, I saw the bodily sight of the plenteous bleeding of the head.

Revelations of Divine Love, ch. 7

For the last three chapters of *Revelations of Divine Love*, Julian has been sharing with us the ghostly or spiritual insight of her first revelation. This has taken us into the depths of the significance of the Passion, the nature of him who suffers on the cross, the presence of the Trinity within the person of Christ and the homely love of God, who reaches down to the deepest depths of our need through the medium of prayer and devotion. Finally, Mary has stood before us as the model and icon of all who respond to Christ's homely loving through revered awe.

The figure of Mary standing before her seems to recall Julian to the scene of the Passion once again, for from ghostly insight we shift back to bodily vision and return to the place of beginning and ending as if for the first time. But now Julian homes in on the great drops of blood that run out from under the garland.

Julian's seamless shift of gear from one sight to another raises pertinent questions about the nature and form of her visions. Are they direct from God, like a message handed down from one angelic personage to a mortal? Or are they shaped and formed in Julian's inner mental and experiential world, expressing truth, yes, but truth mediated through the language, imagery and context of her time and character? It is clear that many visionaries in Julian's day claimed the former; Julian, however, upholds the latter. Despite the fact that Julian erased herself from her text, her words are given to us as a complex interplay of visual record, deeper significance, personal understanding and church teaching. But where one might like to differentiate these into various forms of hermeneutics, Julian condenses them into one showing with various forms.

The key to this reading of Julian's visions can be found in chapter 51. Confused and perplexed by the exemplum of the lord and the servant, Julian asks for help to understand what she has seen. She identifies three properties to this revelation and all the revelations that have been given to her: the first is the beginning of the teaching, namely the visual bodily sight; the second is the inward learning that she subsequently came to have; and the third is the whole revelation 'from the beginning to the end, that is to say, of this book, which our Lord God of his goodness brings oftentimes freely to the sight of my understanding'. The bodily sight; the significance and insight from long meditation; and the written words of the book – these are not subsequent stages in a process of transmitting her vision but different aspects of one revelation.

Just as Julian was bidden by Christ 'to take heed of all the properties and conditions that were shown in the example, though you think them mysterious and indifferent to your sight', so she becomes for us an icon and a model for 'reading' her text, interpretation and vision. Like Julian, we are to use all our wit and understanding to comprehend the meaning and significance of her words for us. Using reason and interpretation is not for Julian a second mode of seeing, as it was for Augustine. Rather, the natural gifts of the mind are as important as that of the open heart. This is very different from other devotional writers of the time, such as the author of *The Cloud of Unknowing*, who famously wrote, 'By love he can be grasped and held, but by thought neither grasped nor held' (chapter 6). In a hierarchy of comprehension, reason and wit are seen as human virtues that are incapable of comprehending God in the cloud that separates us from him. It is only by subsuming reason, thought, meditation, images, even words, however good, under a cloud of forgetting that the contemplative soul is freed to pierce that cloud with a sharp dart of love-longing.

Anyone who has tried to escape the ceaseless meanderings of the mind to enter a deeper stillness will know how difficult this can be. The minute one tries to find inner peace and silence, a cacophony of thoughts, internal dialogue, musings and simple dull nothings disturbs and destroys the inner tranquillity. Techniques of repetition can occupy the verbal recesses of the mind, while the gentle recognition of thoughts that are then let go can help the meditating mind to find a state of being that embraces thoughts but does not let them dictate.

For Julian, reason, thought, meditation, the use of wit and understanding are, like forms of prayer and worship, means to enable the flow of God's gifts of goodness to the deepest recesses of the soul. Like Walter Hilton, Julian sees a God-given role for reason and images that in themselves are able to draw the soul into that deeper response of pure love of which the *Cloud* author speaks. They are not only the means of conveying the love of God to the soul, but they are also the means by which the soul can be inspired and ravished into that state of love which can know him more fully.

In the same way Julian's words and imagery are not only a conduit for her to impart the form and substance of her vision to us the reader, but they are also shaped and moulded by her interpretation and understanding. We are given the vision not as God gave it to Julian but rather as Julian received it in the words, images, ideas and understanding she brought to it. God's revelation of love to Julian is shaped and formed by Julian. But for Julian this does not make it any less valid. Instead, she uses the ideas of her age, cross-referencing and embellishing them, returning to thoughts and images again and again, showing us the revelation from many different angles and aspects so that slowly the truth emerges within our minds and hearts. Letting our minds tease out and think through her words, they then become the means for enabling us to be open to the same revelation of God's love for us as for Julian.

Julian does not want us to yearn to have a spiritual, mystical experience, as if we were a favoured few who were shown some special grace; rather, she wants us to love God better. This is the end of all her writing, and it is important to remember this in order to begin to understand what is happening under the surface of Julian's written text, to which we now turn once again.

Plenteous bleeding of the head

In chapter 7 of *Revelations of Divine Love*, Julian returns once again to the visual, bodily sight of the crown of thorns on Jesus' head. This scriptural image seemed to be subsumed and lost under the weight of its significance and meaning which the intervening chapter expanded and explored. Now Julian refocuses on the garland as she considers the blood that oozes out from under the torturous thorns, but this time she sees with new eyes of understanding and so unfolds new layers of significance:

> The great drops of blood fell down from under the garland like pellets, seemingly as if they had come out of the veins; and in the coming out it was brown red, for the blood was full thick, and in the spreading abroad it was bright red, and when it came to the brows, then it vanished, notwithstanding the bleeding continued till many things were seen and understood.

Time seems to slow down in this sentence as Julian is given time not just to see Christ's bleeding head but to really look and behold with understanding. It is the fruits of this beholding that she imparts to us in her text.

The text itself has a visceral quality to it. The trickles of blood have turned into great droplets that ooze out of the wounds made by the instrument of humiliation. Julian lingers on the form and colour of the blood as it seeps out from under the garland of thorns and runs down his face. But the words and imagery she uses recall not so much the physical encounter with a bleeding head as the visual representations of this scriptural moment in art at the time. The imagery of the crucifixion scene in the Holkham Bible Picture Book (see Plate 10) perfectly expresses Julian's vision of the crown of thorns. Probably written in London during the decades before 1350, this book, which was owned by a Dominican friar and was part of the library at Holkham Hall in Norfolk, encapsulates many of the depictions of the crown of thorns in the late 14th century. Here Jesus' head is upright, the thorns encircle his head and from underneath great droplets of blood are seen to hang like pear drops upon his forehead. Just as Julian saw in her revelation, these droplets congregate like small pellets or packets of blood that have oozed out of the prick of the thorns, thick and dark, then lighter as they spread over his head. Like Julian's description of the blood, so the artist of the picture book depicts the blood as neatly encircling Jesus' head and not covering or enclosing his face.

Compared to late-medieval imagery, the gospel accounts of the crucifixion of Jesus lack the descriptive detail that make it present to the reader's eye. Rather, the gospel writers are terse in their style, recalling the bare facts passed down to them orally by the first apostles and disciples. It is later medieval writers, especially those who sought to evoke an emotional response to the events of the Passion, who included imagined details and theological signifiers that shaped the artistic tropes and iconography of the medieval period. Illustrators of manuscripts such as the Holkham Bible Picture

Book worked within clear theological ideas and understanding of the Passion. Their work was not meant to be artistic for art's sake; it was intended to draw the person who used the image through prayer into a deeper understanding of the significance of the cross and to personally engage with the dying Christ.

Julian's vision was a revelation and gift directly from God, but it was formed and mediated through the language and imagery of a 14th-century understanding and representation of the Passion, as expressed in the art, writing, liturgy, preaching, poetry, plays and so on that made up the devotional culture of the time. What is remarkable about Julian is that, through this prism of the devotional cultural landscape of her day, she sees a multitude of meanings that are new and startling in their depth of significance. This can be seen if we look at the theology that lies behind Julian's description of the blood oozing out from Jesus' crown of thorns. It is the same theology that lies behind the artistic representation of the Passion in the Holkham Bible Picture Book.

The blood of Christ has held deep theological and liturgical significance for Christians throughout history. But in the medieval period, the role of a single drop of Christ's blood came to have particular resonance in what was known as the economy of salvation. In 1264 Pope Urban IV instituted the Feast of Corpus Christi (the Body of Christ), which not only celebrated the real presence of the body and blood of Christ within the bread and wine of the Eucharist but also raised the profile of devotion to them. Hymns that accompanied this feast beautifully expressed the underlying theology of the Passion and the presence. One of these hymns, 'Adoro te devote' by the 13th-century theologian Thomas Aquinas, draws out in particular the precious nature of Jesus' blood, 'one drop of which can free the entire world of all its sins'.

A number of biblical passages lie behind this understanding of the saving power of Christ's blood, not least 1 Peter 1:18–19:

> You know that you were ransomed from the futile ways inherited from your ancestors, not with perishable things like silver or gold, but with the precious blood of Christ, like that of a lamb without defect or blemish.

In both the hymn and Peter's letter, it is the very precious nature of Christ's blood which comes to the fore; just a single drop is able to save the entire world. It was invariably only a single drop, which the devout were able to see in the phials of Christ's blood that were held as relics in both Hailes Abbey and Westminster Abbey. Even the image in Matthew Paris' account, of the holy relic being carried by Henry II in 1247 to Westminster Abbey, depicts the precious phial in the shape of a drop (see Plate 11). Today, the relic of the holy blood is processed through the Basilica of the Holy Blood in Bruges for the faithful to venerate. Like the medieval jar that the king held, this small glass phial holds barely a drop of the precious blood, but that is enough to save the sins of the world.

As in Bruges, so in the medieval world, this precious drop was held in keeping by the church. In artistic representations of the Passion, angels often hover beneath the outstretched arms of Christ on the cross to catch the precious droplets of blood within golden chalices, a visual linking of the blood of Christ with the cup of wine at the Eucharist. The keeper of this holy sacrament is made even more distinct in the Amesbury Missal, where it is Ecclesia herself, Holy Mother Church, who collects the precious drops of Christ's blood. Only one drop of blood is enough to save humanity, but it was only through the church that this economy of salvation was handed out.

Alongside this imagery of devotion to the precious nature of Christ's blood is another evocative, and perhaps more pertinent, biblical reference to the image of droplets of blood. In Luke's gospel, Jesus' agony in the garden of Gethsemane is described in these terms:

> In his anguish he prayed more earnestly, and his sweat became like great drops of blood falling down on the ground.
> LUKE 22:44

For the medieval audience who were using the Latin Vulgate, with all its inaccuracies, this passage would have read in its English translation: 'And his sweat became as drops of blood trickling down upon the ground.' It would not be surprising if this intense image of the agony and suffering of Jesus in the garden, sweating drops of blood, was imaginatively transferred and blended into Julian's description of her vision of the Passion. We cannot say for certain that these images and thoughts lay directly behind the description of her revelation, but the devotional and theological resonances of the words she uses would not have been lost on her medieval audience. Julian, therefore, evokes both the economy of salvation and the agony of Christ in her description of the great drops that she sees falling from under the garland of thorns. What is interesting is the way she then develops this imagery and understanding to express new theological and devotional insights.

In chapter 7 Julian moves into interpretive mode in the blink of an eye, even as the vision is unfolding. She describes three aspects to her vision: first, the great drops look like pellets as they ooze from Christ's veins; second, they spread out like the scales of a herring; third, the quantity of blood is like cascading water falling from the eaves after a great shower of rain. These three striking similes are sequential, moving through the vision as it changes and develops. We will look at each of them in turn.

Given the significance of Christ's blood in the culture of her day, as we have just seen, it is striking that Julian articulates her vision in such terms. The word 'pellet' comes from the Old French *pelote* and is based on the Latin *pilotta*, which means a ball or spherical object. The more usual meaning we are familiar with, which is associated with a pellet fired from a gun, was known in the 14th century, as Chaucer uses the word in this sense in his poem 'The House of Fame':

Thrughout every regioun
Wente this foule trumpes soun,
As swifte as pelet out of gonne,
Whan fyr is in the poudre ronne.
'The House of Fame', l. 1,643

Pelote also referred to a pill or bolus of salve that was used to fight the plague. Julian's metaphor to describe how the blood oozed from Christ's wounds is therefore replete with the significance of healing, quantity and roundness. There are also resonances with Julian's image of the world in chapter 5, where she describes all that is made as being like a small ball in the palm of her hand. The whole universe is as small and round as a hazelnut, yet one tiny round ball of blood can redeem it all.

From the beads of blood at the base of the garland, Julian's vision begins to unfold: 'And in the coming out it was brown red, for the blood was full thick; and in the spreading abroad it was bright red.' With remarkable detail she describes not only the way the blood spreads across Jesus' forehead but also the manner in which it changes colour as it does so. Laying aside all the significance and symbolism of Jesus' blood, her description of the way in which it seeps out from the wounds is grounded and rooted in everyday observation. She captures in words exactly what happens to any of us when we prick a finger or cut ourselves. The blood does indeed emerge slowly as a dark red ball, thick and globular, and then flows outwards. It is not insignificant that Julian uses such familiar, everyday descriptive words, for while on one level she is seeing the Passion of Christ, on another level what she beholds is a person who bleeds just like us. In this way Julian roots the historical, devotional events of the Passion within our own everyday human experience.

Julian takes this grounding of the Passion within everyday life still further in describing how the blood in her vision slowly seeped out of the wounds and spread. As many commentators have mentioned, herring was a staple of the medieval diet and abundant in Norwich.

Yarmouth, not far away, was a centre of the fishing industry, and Norwich may well have been so too. Herrings were therefore a regular sight and were probably sold as a whole fish, rather than filleted as they are today. It would have been commonplace to know that the scales of a herring were round, shiny and closely linked. Anyone who has had to clean and prepare a herring will also know that their scales are very numerous and get everywhere. As Julian looks at the bleeding figure of Christ, she is reminded of the very domestic occurrence of descaling herrings and the roundness of their scales. Perhaps she is just trying to paint a word picture for us, so we may imagine for ourselves what she saw herself, but it seems to me that she is doing more than this. She is locating the cross within the sphere of domestic and homely experience.

The final simile Julian uses to describe the blood which flows from Jesus' wounds confirms this notion. As she sees the events of the Passion unfold in minute and intimate terms, the blood seeps from Christ's wounds, slowly spreads across his skin and then drips from his body. The seeping blood is like pellets, spreading out like herring scales, and the dripping reminds her of 'the drops of water that fall from the eaves after a great shower of rain, that fall so thick that no man may number them for bodily understanding'.

In a way, the Holkham Bible Picture Book visualises this dripping blood for us very well, as blood runs down Jesus' arm and simply drips like water from him. But Julian's description differs in two crucial ways: in the homely nature of the scene and in her description of the sheer quantity of blood in her vision.

This image concludes the triptych of domestic simile and needs little explanation. Modern houses do not quite have the same overhanging eaves as medieval buildings had, but visit any of our historic towns or cities, such as Lavenham in Suffolk or Lincoln, York or Norwich, and there are still the remnants of our medieval past scattered and hidden down cobbled backstreets. Again Julian locates her vision within the domestic experience of her medieval readers. Not only can we imagine for ourselves what it is like to see water pouring down after a heavy shower, but the simile also gives us a visceral sense of the quantity of blood which she sees flowing from Jesus' wounds.

At this point in her vision Julian simply describes the plenteous nature of Christ's bleeding, but it is a theme that she will return to and develop through the fourth showing in her revelation (see page 111). Instead, Julian concludes this first showing by returning to the main theme, 'that our Lord, who is so reverent and dreadful, is so homely and courteous'. However, her focus has changed. In chapter 4, it was Julian who spoke in awe at the sight of the garland of thorns being placed on Christ's head. We were invited to make her words our own, to take her prayer of wonder on to our lips, but it was still Julian who marvelled that the most high God, who is so 'reverend' and 'dreadful', would be so familiar or homely with a sinful soul like her. Having journeyed with her through her complex engagement with her vision, which has focused on the domesticity of God's enfolding us with love, pouring out his goodness to us through prayer and setting Mary as an icon of this familial relationship that we are invited to have with Christ, Julian finally, through everyday domestic images, locates the events of the Passion within the reader's sphere of understanding and experience. This is not a showing of a past event which we have to imagine ourselves back into. Rather, it is the pouring out of Christ's blood and love in a present event. Julian has folded time so that the Passion is a living reality to us, and she has also placed us into the space she occupied as the recipient of her vision.

Chapter 7 concludes with a parable, which is not only an exemplum of homely love but also acts as a bridging device, transferring Julian's focus on to the reader. It is the final piece in her series of domestic, everyday images, which places the Passion and the humble love of God into the sphere of experience of the medieval reader. The example clearly has overtones of the biblical parables of Jesus, which speak of a lord and a servant, but especially where Jesus says:

> Blessed are those slaves whom the master finds alert when he comes; truly I tell you, he will fasten his belt and have them sit down to eat, and he will come and serve them.
>
> LUKE 12:37

In the post-feudal culture of the 14th century, when the language of courtesy and lordship still shaped the social discourse and conventions, the biblical imagery of the lord–servant relationship was more easily translatable than it is in ours today. The example reads:

> It is the most worshipful thing that a solemn king or great lord may do for a poor servant if he will be homely with him, and namely if he acts in this way himself, full of true meaning and with a glad cheer, both privately and openly. Then thinks this poor creature so: 'Ah! What might his noble lord do that is more honourable and joyous to me than to show me, that am so simple, this marvellous intimacy? Truly it is more joy and favourable to me than if he gave me great gifts and were himself strange in his manner.'

In this short example Julian condenses the essence of the meaning of the first showing and distils it into an image which the medieval reader would have easily related to. It takes the insight her vision has given her into the truly humble and self-giving nature of Jesus on the cross and places it in the life and experience of her medieval reader. Though Jesus Christ is our Lord and Saviour, through his familial act of self-giving love, he becomes intimately involved with his servants and enters their everyday, ordinary lives. The prayer that Julian herself cried out in utter awe and wonder is now transferred into an example which the reader may truly say and own for themselves. So Julian states that this bodily example was shown 'so high that men's hearts might be ravished and almost forget themselves for joy and his great homeliness'. Drawing on the language of mystical encounter, Julian places her vision into our hands and allows us to stand in the place where she has stood and be lost in wonder, love and praise.

Going deeper

As you read Julian's visionary words, once again allow your imagination to paint a picture in your mind's eye.

> The great drops of blood fell down from under the garland like pellets, seemingly as if they had come out of the veins; and in the coming out it was brown red, for the blood was full thick; and in the spreading abroad it was bright red; and when it came to the brows, then it vanished, notwithstanding the bleeding continued till many things were seen and understood.

What associations do these words have for you?

How does this make you feel?

Allowing your inner thoughts and feelings to float away like clouds across the moon, come to a place of wonder, love and praise.

What will you take away with you from this time of meditation?

Questions to ponder or discuss

- How do you understand the nature and purpose of visions?
- Where do you see God working in daily life?
- What does the Eucharist mean for you?
- What does it mean for you to be served by Christ?
- Whose feet will you wash this week?

Words for the journey

> How much more will the blood of Christ, who through the eternal Spirit offered himself without blemish to God, purify our conscience from dead works to worship the living God!
>
> HEBREWS 9:14

*

The second revelation

– 7 –

THE FACE OF JESUS

Julian gives a powerful description of Jesus' face. This chapter muses on the seeming withdrawal of God, what it is that makes him inaccessible or lost to us in our lives. Biblical parallels are drawn with one of Jesus' last sayings on the cross, 'Father, forgive them.' Drawing on Julian's teaching on prayer it dwells on the idea of seeking and finding.

And after this I saw with bodily sight in the face of the crucifix that hung before me, in which I beheld continually aspects of his Passion: despite, spitting, defilement, buffeting and many languishing pains more than I can tell, and often changing of colour.

Revelations of Divine Love, ch. 10

Julian's description of her second revelation begins in the most disarming way. We would not even know that this was her second revelation if the chapter summary beforehand had not set the scene. If Julian had not given us this rubric, we would have been most confused, for the chapter begins mid-sentence: 'And after this...' After what? It is as if Julian has wandered off in an aside for the past couple of chapters and now brings us right back to her vision once again by refocusing our attention on the physical wooden crucifix which the priest held before her eyes at her bedside.

However, this time her vision has developed, and we are no longer bidden to concentrate on the crown of thorns which encircled Jesus' head but rather on his face, which shifted and changed before her eyes in an uneasy and destabilising way. Unlike the first revelation, which spread across a number of chapters, her second revelation is contained within one chapter, chapter 10, which acts as a self-contained unit both structurally and emotionally, moving the reader from a place of anxiety, instability and general chaos to structured reassurance, concluding with an outburst of adoration. In this way the shape and feel of the chapter echoes its content, which addresses the shifting pattern of the hiddenness and presence of Jesus within the devotional life.

At the beginning of chapter 10, the face of Jesus is very much present to Julian through the carved image of the crucifix. We cannot tell for certain exactly what type of cross it was that the priest held before Julian's eyes, though it probably contained an image of Christ. Most of the crosses that survive from this period have some figurative representation of the image of Jesus, and it is on the person of Jesus that Julian's revelation pivots. Even very poorly made wooden crosses would have sought to evoke a response to the person of Jesus who died on a cross. This was even more important during last rites, which Julian had received prior to her vision, when the representation of the suffering Christ, the man of sorrows, sought to evoke a deep emotional response in the dying person in order to encourage them to make a true and heartfelt confession. The sight of he who bore their sins on the cross was a powerful incentive to 'seek the Lord while he is near', for soon it would be too late. It is within this acute penitential atmosphere that we approach Julian's description of the second revelation.

Disfigured by violence

As Julian looked on the face of Jesus on the wooden crucifix, her vision of the Passion continued to unfold. From the crowning with thorns, it shifted to focus on the other acts of violence Jesus suffered at the hands of the Roman soldiers. To capture this visceral experience, Julian codifies these events in her text into single words which contain the emotional essence of the narrative of the Passion within them. Like the artistic symbols of the Passion that surround the Despenser Retable in Norwich Cathedral, each word is replete with meaning and captures the horrific events of the narrative:

1 *Despite*: 'They put a reed in his right hand and knelt before him and mocked him' (Matthew 27:29).
2 *Spitting*: 'They spat on him' (Matthew 27:30).
3 *Defilement*: 'They stripped him' (Matthew 27:28).
4 *Buffeting*: 'They... struck him on the head' (Matthew 27:30).

Like slaps across the face, each word rains down a concentrated strike of images and ideas that not only evoke a deeper emotive response from the reader but also invite an imaginative expansion of the word through personal meditation. These single powerful words, along with the implied continuation that concludes them ('and many languishing pains, more than I can tell'), force the reader to look again at the Passion narrative and to imaginatively and emotionally encounter the suffering and humiliation of Jesus for themselves in a very personal and intimate way through the mutilation of his face.

Veiled by blood

Where time had sped up with the condensing of the narrative of Jesus' humiliation into a quantum of action words, now time slows right down as Julian's description expresses the effect these beatings had on the face of Jesus:

> And one time I saw how half the face, beginning at the ear, overspread with dried blood till it enclosed to the middle of the face, and after that, the other half enclosed in the same manner, and meanwhile in the first part as before.

For us today who have the means of alleviating much of the suffering that our ancestors could only but endure, to linger on the lacerations of Jesus seems gruesomely manipulative and morally repugnant. But the sight of broken bodies and bloodied wounds, along with the reality of living with pain, was perhaps more normative in Julian's day than in our own, especially for a generation who had lived through the grim reality of the Black Death. In a cultural climate that is both appalled at the physical mutilation we see happening across the world and yet also entertained by gory violence on TV and film, the idea of approaching the physicality of the crucifixion of Jesus as a devotional practice can at best leave mixed feelings.

For the medieval mind, however, it was this very physicality that bridged the human, visceral experience of daily life and suffering with the divine, embodied and very human person of Christ. His wounds and blood witnessed to the incarnate God, who suffered in the same fragile body as us all. To meditate on the fractured and bloodied wounds of Christ was not to relish in suffering or ghoulishly delight in torture but to bring one closer to the overwhelming reality that God willingly suffered and died as a real human being out of love for his broken, sinful creation.

It is perhaps for this very reason that Julian's second revelation lingers on the slow spread of blood from one side of Jesus' face to the other. Julian was not alone among devotional writers of her day in focusing on the disfigurement of Jesus' face during the events of his Passion. The words she uses to describe the experience of her second revelation are much akin to those of a contemporary devotional writer, Richard Rolle. Like Julian, Rolle, in his *Meditations on the Passion*, describes Jesus' face as being 'so pale and so swollen with buffeting and with beating, with spitting, with spouting blood'. Julian was therefore writing into and out of a well-trodden path of language and images used in meditations on the Passion. In both cases the focus is on describing the effects of the Passion on the 'lovely face' of Jesus, or, as Rolle puts it, the disfigurement of the true image of Christ. Where the devotional images and meditations of her day sought to evoke an emotional response of compassion and pity to the man of sorrows, in Julian's vision the lovely face of Jesus slowly receded from her sight until it became hidden, obscured behind a veil of blood.

The withdrawal of Christ

Julian documents her reaction to this slow withdrawal of Jesus, as one side of his face is slowly covered with dried blood and then the other: 'This saw I bodily, sorrowfully and darkly, and I desired more bodily sight to have seen more clearly.' On one level Julian is simply stating the effect the vision had on her and its bewildering nature, but on another level her desire to see more clearly indicates a spiritual yearning that has stretched down through the ages. From psalmist to prophet the cry has gone out: 'Why do you hide your face?' (Psalm 44:24); 'Why, O Lord, do you stand far off?' (Psalm 10:1). The psalmist laments the sense of separation he feels from a now distant God: 'O Lord, by Your favour You have made my mountain to stand strong; You hid Your face, I was dismayed' (Psalm 30:7, NASB). The answer to these questions was clear to the prophets who spoke the word of the Lord to the wayward people of God: 'According to their uncleanness and according to their transgressions I dealt with them, and I hid My face from them' (Ezekiel 39:24, NASB). The same idea is found in Isaiah: 'Because of the iniquity of his unjust gain I was angry and struck him; I hid My face and was angry, and he went on turning away, in the way of his heart' (Isaiah 57:17, NASB). Yet just as the Lord withdrew from the presence of his people, he could also give the promise of revealing his face to them once again: 'Although the Lord has given you bread of privation and water of oppression, He, your Teacher will no longer hide Himself, but your eyes will behold your Teacher' (Isaiah 30:20, NASB), and '"I will not hide My face from them any longer, for I will have poured out My Spirit on the house of Israel," declares the Lord God' (Ezekiel 39:29, NASB).

This understanding of God as one who willingly withdraws from his people because of his anger and disgust at their behaviour reflects the often volatile relationship between the people of God and their Lord in the Old Testament. It is very different from the other understanding of the hiddenness of God we find within the Old Testament, which results naturally from his awesome and numinous nature. It is because of the majesty and mystery of God that he resides within a cloud on Mount Sinai, present with but hidden from his people. Only Moses is permitted to see the Lord, but even then only from behind, for 'you cannot see my face; for no one shall see me and live' (Exodus 33:20).

It is this aspect of the numinous and mysterious nature of God that we most often associate with the writings of the mystics. They are the ones who claim to pierce the cloud and look beyond the veil into the holy of holies. But there was also a series of texts in the 14th century that sought to explain the very fluctuating experience of God in the ordinary spiritual lives of the devout. The anonymously written *The Chastising of God's Children* and William Flete's *Remedies against Temptations* were both composed towards the end of the 14th century for a burgeoning devout laity, to speak into some of their concerns. One of these concerns was the sense of disparity between feeling very near to God one minute and then the next minute feeling abandoned and distant from God, who was seemingly hidden and remote. It is a question that is still asked by many today, regardless of how long a person may have walked the spiritual path.

St John of the Cross famously gave us the insight of the 'dark night of the soul' in the 16th century to explain the dereliction that a soul felt in those wilderness moments. Two centuries earlier, the 14th-century tribulation texts, as they are known today, used a very different image to explain the withdrawal of God from his beloved: that of motherhood. The author of *The Chastising of God's Children* sought to reassure the struggling soul, who felt that her sinfulness was to blame for the seeming withdrawal of their Lord, by depicting God as a mother playing with her child, sometimes being present and sometimes absent. In her absence the heart hardens and the body becomes sluggish so that the child is 'like to fall into vices', but yet she 'loves us nevertheless'. The author makes a clear difference between the feeling that the soul is to blame for the disappearance of the mother and the reality of the mother's forgiveness. The mother is an abiding, though hidden, presence.

The author gives four reasons why the mother withdraws from her children. The first and the third are connected with penance and the protection of the soul through the life of virtue: to prevent pride and to stop presumption. The second reason is so that the soul may know its weakness and need of its mother, and the fourth reason is in order that the soul may seek after God as a child does its mother. In each case God does not withdraw herself from her beloved child out of punishment for sinfulness, but rather for the child's spiritual good and even to excite that desire which leads the soul to seek after God. It is this devotional desire which we see reflected in Julian's response to the slow withdrawal of the lovely face of Jesus behind a mask of blood. Like the moment when a loved one, receding from view, ignites an overwhelming desire to see and touch them once again, so Jesus' withdrawal behind the curtain of blood ignites Julian's desire to see more.

Walking by faith

Julian's plea to see more clearly is answered through these words: 'If God will show thee more, he shall be thy light. You need none but him.' Often within her revelation, Julian hears the voice of Jesus speaking to her, which she then records in her text through the use of direct speech. Here, however, she tells us that her wish to see more clearly was not answered by another bodily sight or divine locution, but rather within her own reasoning. The answer that is formed in her head is, nonetheless, rooted and grounded in scripture. The imagery of light within scripture is well attested; it is a theme which runs through the heart of the terminology for the Lord both in the Old Testament – 'The Lord is my light and my salvation' (Psalm 27:1) – and in the New, where Christ is named as 'the true light, which enlightens everyone' (John 1:9), to highlight but two verses out of many.

It is also a prevalent theme through Julian's writings. Much later in the long text Julian gives us an insight into her understanding and development of imagery of God as light, which illuminates our understanding of this statement at this point in her text. In chapter 83 she describes God as having three distinct properties: life, love and light. These relate to the three persons of the Trinity: life as the homeliness of the Father, which we have already seen in chapter 5; love of the gentle courtesy of the Son, which is expressed through the motherhood of Christ; and light, the kindling fire of the Holy Spirit. At this point in her text, Julian directly associates the image of light with the work of the Holy Spirit. As the image of Jesus withdraws, she is reminded that the light of Christ shines in our hearts through the presence of the Holy Spirit. It is this light of the Holy Spirit that not only kindles the desire and enflames our hearts with love but is also the light by which we can walk even when Christ our light seems to have withdrawn from us.

Julian's own exuberance and desire for God, expressed in the language of desire, is witnessing to the theological truth that even when Jesus is obscured by darkness, the light of the Holy Spirit still enflames the heart that we may be assured of God's presence even in his seeming absence. For Julian this light of the Holy Spirit is given to us directly by God as our faith:

> Our faith is a light, naturally proceeding from our endless day that is our Father, God; in which light our mother, Christ, and our good Lord the Holy Ghost leads us in this passing life.

Julian sees this light of faith as highly personal, measured out to us just as we need it during those times of darkness: 'Our faith is our light in our night; which light is God our endless day.' Faith is thereby not a feeling or faculty that the soul has or has not, but rather is the gift of the presence of God in the soul through the Holy Spirit. We can walk by the light of faith even if we do not experience visions or the overwhelming presence of Christ. Julian is therefore telling herself a truth she already knows, that she does not need to have any more visions or bodily showings because God the Trinity is her light. Unlike her visionary counterparts on the continent, English anchoresses were dissuaded from having visions. The 13th-century guide for anchoresses, the *Ancrene Wisse*, advises: 'Regard any vision you may see, whether in dreams or waking, as mere delusion, for it is nothing but guile.' It is therefore not surprising that in the short text Julian leaves the subject there. After many years of musing on her showings, Julian decides no longer to leave the subject at these words but rather adds a substantial section to her long text, which explores in more depth the devotional experience of the hiddenness of God.

The presence of Christ

At this point Julian steps back once again from the form and substance of her showing to reflect on her relationship with God: 'For I saw him and sought him.' From this phrase, which summarises her response to the revelation, Julian comes to realise the depth to which it is God who seeks out the soul. The initiative so often lies with him rather than us, 'for we are so blind and so unwise that we never seek God till he of his goodness shows himself to us'. Therefore the night of which she talks is not an external objectively evil force but rather all those things that blind us to the light of faith in Christ and extinguish the fire of love in our hearts. It is this blindness that causes us woe and suffering and prevents us from seeing Christ. For Julian, God seems hidden or absent not because this is God's will but because our sight is obscured and dimmed. In contrast it is Christ who is seen as always seeking us out. Julian sees Jesus as the active one in the relationship with the soul, always seeking to bring the soul to his light and life and presence.

Furthermore, once the soul has been seen and found by God, something fundamental happens within it – it is changed. Julian's text bears close similarity to the language of love that we find in other devotional, mystical writers of the times, like Richard Rolle.

In his partly autobiographical *Incendium Amoris*, he opens with the words:

> I cannot tell you how surprised I was the first time I felt my heart begin to warm. It was a real warmth too, not imaginary, and it felt as if I was actually on fire. I was astonished at the way the heat surged up, and how this new sensation brought great and unexpected comfort... But once I realised that it came entirely from within, that this fire of love had no cause, material or sinful, but was the gift of my Maker, I was absolutely delighted, and wanted my love to be even greater.

Julian is perhaps not quite as colourful or ecstatic as Rolle, but her words express the similar notion of the heart being enflamed when it is found and touched by God:

> We ought to seek him graciously, then are we stirred by the same grace to seek with great desire to see him more blissfully, and thus I saw him and sought him, and I had him and I wanted him.

Where Rolle uses the language of love, Julian speaks in terms of desire. This is not something the soul can initiate or manufacture; rather it is the effect of God finding and seeing the soul, which then stirs the soul to seek and desire God in turn, to reciprocate the same love and desire that God has for the soul.

Julian concludes this short devotional excursus with a visual summary of what her thoughts mean in relation to the hiddenness of Christ behind the veil of blood. The image is formed in her understanding and probably based on Psalm 139:9–10:

> If I take the wings of the morning and settle at the farthest limits of the sea, even there your hand shall lead me, and your right hand shall hold me fast.

Without a Bible to scrutinise every word of scripture, Julian instead recalls images and ideas that she has heard and seen. So often within her text Julian speaks the language of scripture rather than quotes it. The same is the case here:

> One time my understanding was led down into the bottom of the sea, and there I saw green hills and dales, as it were overgrown with moss, wreckage and gravel. Then I understood thus that if a man or woman were under the broad water, if he might have sight of God so, that God is with humanity continually, he should be safe in body and soul and take no harm and overpassing, he should have more solace and comfort than all this world can tell; for he wills that we believe that we see him continually, though we think that it be but little, and in this belief he makes us evermore to receive grace; for he will be seen and he will be sought, he will be abided and he will be trusted.

Julian ends with this wonderful passage of comfort, which brings together the main themes of the chapter so far: seeing, believing, grace, seeking, all of which culminate in the words 'abide' and 'trust'. For Julian the hiddenness of God and the pain this causes the soul is not a childish game but a serious concern for those who love and seek God. Neither is it a wilful turning away by a God who is disgusted and angry at our sinfulness. Rather, Julian asserts that, even though we may feel lost and abandoned, this is not the reality of our relationship with God. It is our blindness that masks the love of God, which can only be known through his grace and which enflames our hearts to seek him and desire him. When all is dark, in this we can trust and abide.

Wele and *woe*

Given the affirmation and confidence of the last passage, it seems tragic that, even as Julian affirms this insight into the presence of God with the soul, at the very next moment she is plunged into despair and riddled with doubts about the validity of her revelation:

> This second showing was so low and so little and so simple that my spirits were in great travail in the beholding, mournful, dreadful and longing; for I was sometime in doubt whether it was a showing.

In the first revelation there was an equivalent shift of gravity. However, this time it is reversed. For as Julian looked at the cross and was suddenly lightened in her heart to see the presence of the Trinity, now she moves from an equally illuminated insight into the presence of the light of the Trinity in our lives to the horror and fearful doubt that this revelation may be untrue. This sudden shift from *wele* to *woe* (from joy to sorrow) encapsulates the very problem about which Julian has been speaking and expresses the age-old problem of the power of our emotions to shift, thereby buffeting the soul between states of experience. Julian is given more insight by God in order to reassure her that her revelation is not false, but this unreliable oscillation leads Julian into the next section of her chapter, which focuses on what causes our blindness and obscures our sight and knowledge of the presence of God, robbing us of that comfort and solace that God gives.

The foul, dead covering

Julian understands her experience of slipping from *wele* to *woe* as a visible, tangible expression of 'our foul, dead covering that our fair, bright, blessed Lord bore for our sins'. It is this which causes our blindness and obscures our knowledge of the unending presence of God with us. But what do these words mean? To fully understand the highly evocative and significant meaning of these words for Julian, we need to turn to another place in her writing where, out of a similar experience of *wele* and *woe*, she reflects on the consequences of our human condition.

In chapter 64 of *Revelations of Divine Love*, Julian considers the troubles of this world, not least the perceived absence of God. In response to her overwhelming sense of her own misery and inability to delight in this life, God gives her words of comfort and sows seeds of patience. Using language rooted in 1 Thessalonians 4:17, he reassures her that, in an instant and without warning, this *woe* will turn into *wele* as she will be taken from this world and shall come up above, where there is no manner of pain and sickness. Till then it is the Lord's delight that she patiently abide.

The reasons behind this sudden transformation from *woe* to *wele* are then explained in the visual form of a showing. Julian sees a body lying on the earth which is heavy and ugly, without shape or form, as if it were a swollen mass of entrails of stinking mire. Suddenly from this body Julian sees a beautiful child spring forth. It is a fair creature, like a child all fully formed, lively and active, whiter than a lily. Julian explains this image:

> The distension of the body betokened the great wretchedness of our deadly flesh, and the littleness of the child betokens the cleanness of purity in the soul.

The two could not be more sharply contrasted: a seething quagmire of entrails and a beautifully formed child. The soul was often represented in art as a young child, issuing like a spirit from a person's mouth up to heaven at the point of death. However, this is not to say that the contrast between the pure childlike spirit and the stinking mass of flesh represents the dualistic divide between the body and the soul, as often expressed by theologians. For Julian the heavy and ugly body is not the physical body created by God out of the mud to form Adam, but is rather the misery of our mortal flesh.

In his letter to the Romans, Paul describes two states of being, one of the flesh and the other of the spirit. These two states he describes as pulling us apart and causing great misery:

> When I want to do what is good, evil lies close at hand. For I delight in the law of God in my inmost self, but I see in my members another law at war with the law of my mind, making me captive to the law of sin that dwells in my members. Wretched man that I am! Who will rescue me from this body of death? Thanks be to God through Jesus Christ our Lord.
>
> ROMANS 7:21–25

Paul's answer to his question is Jesus, who clothes himself in the 'likeness of sinful flesh, and to deal with sin, he condemned sin in the flesh, so that the just requirement of the law might be fulfilled in us, who walk not according to the flesh but according to the Spirit' (Romans 8:3–4). For Julian, the quagmire of unformed chaos is therefore not an image of a battle between the physical body and the soul; she is not advocating a retreat from this earthly life to the joys of heaven. Rather it is the warring chaos of the flesh, which fragments our lives, obscures our sight of God and causes us to be wretched. Julian expresses this state within herself when she recognises that it is her own wretchedness, laziness and weakness that make her want to escape the suffering of this world to be taken up to the joys of heaven.

Similarly, the child is not an image of the inner purity and cleanness of the soul as released from the body; instead it represents the life of the Spirit through the incarnation and Passion of Christ, who condemned sin in his own flesh. As Paul writes, 'For you have died, and your life is hidden with Christ in God' (Colossians 3:3). Julian tells us then to set our minds on this 'courteous promise of clean deliverance', just as Paul tells us to set our minds 'on things that are above' (Colossians 3:2), where Christ is.

With pity not blame

Julian's notion of the wretchedness and misery of this mortal life has great implications for her understanding of the fall, which differs markedly from that of Paul and the given theology of her day. Unlike the standard Augustinian teaching of the time, which taught that the fall resulted from a wilful act of disobedience against God, Julian follows Anselm, who figured the fall as an error, a mishap that plunged humanity into a state where it could no longer see God but focused only on its own suffering. Julian knows the teaching of the church, that the blame of sin hangs on us from the time of Adam, but her revelation has shown that God shows us no blame. She therefore asks God to show her how he looks on us in our sin, and in reply God gives her an extended exemplum, which she describes in chapter 53.

The example is a figurative representation of the story of the fall, but it differs markedly from the Old Testament narrative, being couched in the parables of Jesus, in the theology of Anselm and in feudal law. Instead of disobedience being the core motivation for the fall, Julian describes the intimate relationship between a lord and his servant who, out of love, runs off to do the bidding of his lord. In his haste he accidentally falls into a ditch and is sorely hurt:

> Then he groans and moans and twists and writhes, but he may not rise nor help himself by no possible way. And of all this the most mischief that I saw him in was failing of comfort; for he could not turn his face to look upon his loving lord, which was to him full near, in whom is full comfort but as a man that was feeble and unwise for the time he attended to his feeling and endured in woe, in which woe he suffered seven great pains.

For nearly 20 years Julian considers all the points of this example and comes to realise that the lord is God and the servant is Adam, or everyman, who was hurt in his strength, made weak and stunned in his understanding and who can no longer see God. For Julian this changeable mortality of our existence makes us have a propensity to sin, for he is 'unmighty and unwise of himself and also his will is overlaid; and in this time he is in tempest and in sorrow and woe, and the cause is blindness, for he does not see God' (chapter 47).

This is the sad state of the flesh, in which we all find ourselves. It is the 'deadly covering', which our Lord bore for our sins.

Julian chooses her words carefully here. The 'fair bright blessed Lord', echoing the purity of the soul, places or robes himself in our flesh, that 'stinking mass of suffering', for our sins. The 'foul, dead covering' is not sin itself but rather the state which makes us liable, open and weak to sin.

Sin is nothing

For Julian, sin is therefore not an action or a substance. It is not like the wilful transgression we pray forgiveness for each time we say the Lord's Prayer. Instead, she sees sin as an absence, a non-entity. We know sin only by the effect it has on us. Sin thereby causes wounds that further weaken us, causing suffering and further blindness. So in her exemplum, Julian comes to see the figure of the servant as not just Adam but also representing Christ, who robes himself in the 'white kirtle' of human flesh. This bodily garment is clean and bright. It is not our bodies that are evil or sinful. For Julian, it is through falling into the death of the quagmire of this world that the garments are dirtied and rent. Just as Adam fell into the mire of death, so Christ fell into the maiden's womb to share in the condition of this earthly life. Christ's 'white kirtle' is torn and rent, just as his fair and beautiful face is slashed and mutilated by the humiliation and flagellation of the soldiers:

> Be that his kirtle was in detail to be ragged and rent is understood the whips and the scourges, the thorns and the nails, the drawing and the dragging, his tender flesh rending; as I saw in some part, the flesh was rent from the skull, falling in pieces into the time the bleeding failed; and then it began to dry again, clinging to the bone. And by the wallowing and writhing, groaning and moaning, is understood that he might never rise all mightily from the time he was fallen in to the

> maiden's womb till his body was slain and dead, he yielding the soul in the Father's hands with all mankind for whom he was sent.

Thus in her second revelation Julian sees the 'fair and blessed' face of Jesus receding behind the 'foul, deadly covering' in which Christ willingly enfolds himself for our sin. Just as Julian saw the Lord enfolding us in robes of love in her first revelation, so now in her second revelation Christ is depicted as wrapping himself in the covering of our foul and deadly flesh to take on himself the consequences of sin for sheer love.

Going deeper

Give yourself some time to linger on these words by Julian. What do they mean for you?

> For I saw him and sought him; for we are so blind and so unwise that we never seek God till he of his goodness shows himself to us. We ought to seek him graciously, then are we stirred by the same grace to seek with great desire to see him more blissfully, and thus I saw him and sought him, and I had him and I wanted him.

What in your life hinders you from knowing God's love?

Where does God reveal himself to you most clearly?

How can you cultivate an attitude of seeking?

Acknowledging your inner thoughts and feelings, allow them to settle, to bring you to a place of watching and waiting and of stillness before your loving Lord.

What will you take away with you from this time of meditation?

Questions to ponder or discuss

- How do you respond to the violence of the cross?
- Why do you think God feels absent in the times when we seemingly most need him?
- What does faith mean for you?
- How would you define sin to someone else?
- How can you reveal the presence of Christ to others this week?

Words for the journey

> Set your minds on things that are above, not on things that are on earth, for you have died, and your life is hidden with Christ in God.
>
> COLOSSIANS 3:2–3

1 The medieval rood screen at St Helen's Church, Ranworth, Norwich

2 Detail of the medieval rood screen at St Helen's Church, Ranworth, Norwich

3 Last rites panel in the seven sacrament window of St Michael's Church, Doddiscombsleigh, Devon

4 Fifteenth-century crucifix

5 The Holy Thorn Reliquary

6 Crown of thorns, detail of the Despenser Retable, Norwich Cathedral

7 The Despenser Retable, Norwich Cathedral

dominus
domino meo:
sede a dex
tris meis.
Donec ponam inimicos tuos: scabel
lum pedum tuorum.
Virgam virtutis tue emittet dominus
ex syon: dominare in medio inimi
corum tuorum.
Tecum principium in die virtutis
tue: in splendoribus sanctorum ex
utero. ante luciferum genui te.

8 Throne of Grace, from the Carrow Psalter

9 Christ holding a globe, detail of the Westminster Retable

10 The Crucifixion, from the Holkham Bible Picture Book

11 The procession of the phial of Christ's blood in the Matthew Paris Chronicle

12 The veil of Veronica, detail of the Despenser Retable, Norwich Cathedral

13 The flagellation of Christ, from the Holkham Bible Picture Book

14 The Vision of Saint Bernard

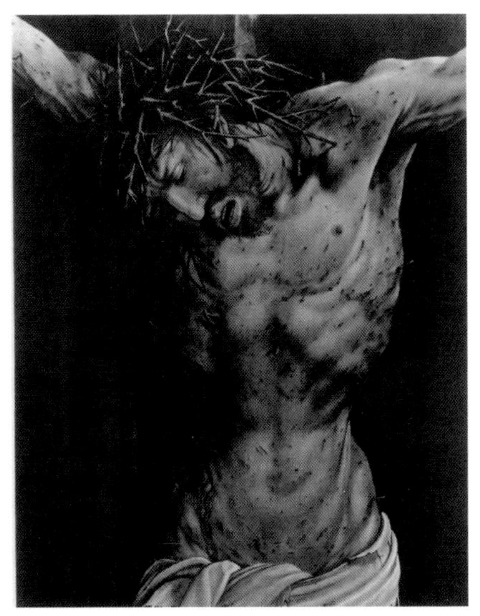

15 The dying Jesus, detail of the Isenheim Altarpiece

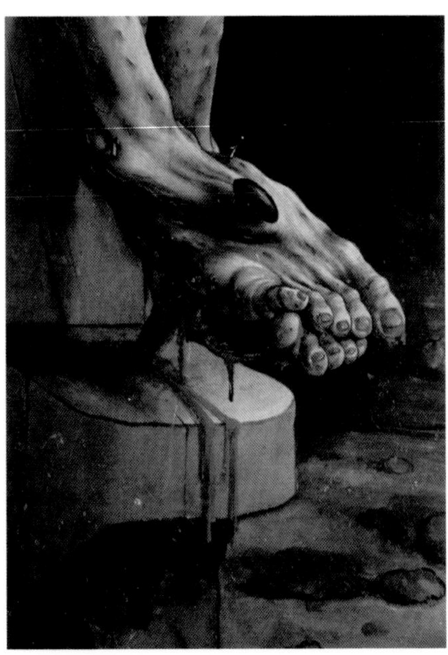

16 Christ's foot, detail of the Isenheim Altarpiece

– 8 –

THE VEIL OF VERONICA

Continuing Julian's exploration of the face of Jesus, this chapter focuses on seeing his true likeness in the medieval relic of the veil of Veronica and the spiritual path of seeing and beholding.

As Julian looks on the face of Jesus, which is slowly encased within the blood of this mortal flesh, she is reminded of a holy relic, the veil of Veronica, known as the vernicle:

> It made me think of the holy vernicle of Rome, which he hath portrayed with his own blessed face when he was in his hard Passion, wilfully going to his death, and often changing in colour.

People in the medieval period believed they knew exactly what Jesus looked like because of the imprint of his blood upon the veil of Veronica. Today the story of Veronica is largely known through the Stations of the Cross, where her tender act of compassion is recorded as the sixth moment in the Via Dolorosa. When she opened the cloth which she had used to wipe his face, Jesus' image was miraculously imprinted upon it. It soon became an important relic; to look on the vernicle was to see the actual face of Jesus imprinted upon cloth in the blood and sweat of his Passion.

Another legend relating to the veil of Veronica brings out this sense of representing the true face of Jesus in even stronger terms to that of its creation on the Via Dolorosa. The popular *Golden Legend*, a collection of stories and miracles on the lives of the saints, by

Jacobus de Voragine, which dates to around 1260, tells the story of Jesus purposefully imprinting an image of his face on to a piece of cloth as a special favour to Veronica, who had wanted to paint his portrait. This legend, along with the story of Veronica wiping the bleeding face of Christ on his way to the cross, left a strong impression on the medieval mind that in this relic was seen the only true likeness of the face of Jesus as created by himself.

The vernicle, or *sudarium*, was therefore always seen as an object of devotion, but this was heightened in 1216 by Pope Innocent III, who offered a ten-day indulgence – a reprieve from the time a soul had to suffer in Purgatory – to anyone who recited the prayer he had composed in honour of the image. In comparison to the 12,000-year indulgence one received for actually seeing the vernicle with one's eyes and making an act of devotion to it, this was a small token, but it still increased devotion to the holy image across Christendom. It is unlikely that Julian would have ever been on pilgrimage to Rome and seen the vernicle with her own eyes, but by this time the veil of Veronica was widely venerated. During the 14th century, the office for the Holy Face was widespread, as were reproductions of the image in books of hours and among the instruments of the Passion. It is even found on the frame of the Despenser Retable in Norwich Cathedral (see Plate 12). In these icons of devotion, the face is rarely shown as a bloodied outline of impressions and blotches, as you would expect from a wiped imprint and as shown on the dubious Turin shroud; rather the vernicle gives the notion that here you see the true and beautiful image of the face of Christ, outlined in his dark blood. However, there was also a tradition associated with the *sudarium* that related to the strange and changeable nature of the image itself, which Julian also expresses in her writing.

The vernicle had a long tradition of appearing dark, deep brown, grey or even black, but it was also thought to hold strange and miraculous properties. For when one looked upon it, the image was often unfixed and altered. It was believed in medieval times that Pope Innocent increased devotion to the relic because of an incident of divine displeasure. While he was processing with the veil from St Peter's Basilica to the Hospital of the Holy Spirit, the face of the image suddenly turned upside down. It was to soften this sign of displeasure that the Pope increased devotion to the cloth. It is these two aspects, the dark colour and the changeableness of the image, that Julian is reminded of when she looks on the face of Jesus on the cross receding behind a veil of blood:

> It made me think of the holy vernicle of Rome, which he hath portrayed with his own blessed face when he was in his hard Passion, wilfully going to his death, and often changing in colour. Of the brown and blackness, piteousness and thinness of this image, many marvel how it might be, considering he portrayed it with his blessed face which is the fairness of heaven, flower of earth and the fruit of the maiden womb. Then how might this image be so discoloured and so far from fair?

In this description we can see these two aspects of the vernicle legend, which her vision brought to mind: the notion that it was imprinted during the time of his Passion and the idea that it expresses not only the hard pains of the Passion in its black and piteous representation but also the strange quality of the constant changing of colour. But within this legend of the vernicle, as well as in her own vision, Julian comes across a basic incongruity: if this image is a true likeness of Christ, which he himself gave us, then why does it not express him in all his beauty and blessedness? Why is it so discoloured and so 'far from fair'?

Far from fair

In some ways, given all that has gone before in her preceding chapters, this is a strange question to ask. But Julian is as astute as ever and has realised that there is a difference between the vernicle and her second revelation. The face of Jesus that has been shown to her in her revelation is the fair, bright blessed face of the Lord, which is slowly covered over by the dried blood of his hard Passion. This visage is hidden, but not soiled and ugly. The vernicle, on the other hand, shows the 'true image' of the face of Christ through the blood of his labour, and it is dark and ugly. How can this be?

Julian gains her understanding of this not from another revelation or even a divine locution but rather from the teachings of the church:

> We know in our faith and believe by the teaching and preaching of holy church that the blessed Trinity made mankind in his image and in his likeness. In the same manner wise we know that when man fell so deep and so wretchedly by sin there was none other to help to restore man but through his that was made man. And that man was made out of love, by the same love he would restore man to the same bliss and more. And just as we were made like to the Trinity in our first making, our maker would that we should be like Jesus Christ our Saviour, in heaven without end, by virtue of our remaking. Then between these two he would, for love and worship of man, make himself as like to man in this deadly life, in our foulness and our wretchedness, and man might be without guilt. Whereof it means as said afore: it was the image and likeness of our foul, black, dead covering wherein our fair, bright, blessed Lord God is hidden.

Julian's theology here is firmly based on Anselm's atonement theory of satisfaction, where Christ takes on the form of humanity and suffers death on the cross to pay the price of sin. It is unlikely that Julian would have read Anselm, but rather she would have known of his theology through the devotional culture of her day. Regardless, she still brings a unique aspect to the satisfaction theory by opening the dynamics of the creation and fall of humanity to encompass the whole Trinity. In Julian's sense of the whole Trinity being present in Christ, it is therefore the Trinity who creates humanity in his image and likeness. When Adam fell, there was no one to help restore him but the Trinity who made him. While in Anselm's ransom theology of salvation this inability of man to save himself is couched in legal and feudal terms, Julian uses the language of love.

This is the essential difference between Julian's theology and the standard doctrine of the fall – the motivation behind the Trinity's actions. For Anselm the affront of sin must be justified or satisfied by rights and obligations in accordance with feudal justice, but for Julian, as we saw in her example of a lord and a servant, the motive is solely one of love. This love was the reason God made humanity in the first place, and out of love humanity is safe and restored to bliss. Julian uniquely brings a Trinitarian dimension to the theology of satisfaction. We are made in the likeness of Christ through the birth and death of the second person of the Trinity. So between the first and second making, the Trinity makes himself like humanity in this deathly life.

In a reversal of the idea of man created in the image and likeness of God, Julian explains that to save humanity and restore him to bliss, the Trinity through Christ takes on the likeness of man. This likeness is one of flesh, the wretchedness and blindness of our existence which suffers and is buffeted by blows, humiliated and subject to death: the 'foul, dead covering'. But it must be remembered who takes on this covering, who humbly descends into our mortal lives so liable to sin. It is Jesus Christ, the second person of the Trinity. We may look on the outer likeness of him in our mortal flesh, slashed and mutilated by the suffering of the sins of the world, but hidden and concealed within is the fair, bright, blessed Lord of the Trinity. Notice how Julian has changed her original statement from 'it was a *figure* and likeness of our foul, dead covering that our fair, bright, blessed Lord bore for our sin' to 'it was the *image* and likeness of our foul, black, dead covering wherein our fair, bright, blessed Lord God is hid'. Therefore, to look on the blackened face of Christ, on the vernicle, is to gaze on the face of Christ in the image and likeness of our mortal flesh. However, contained within that image, like the small, pure child, is the nature of the Trinity.

Changing cheer

Having answered the question of why Jesus' true likeness is so discoloured, Julian now addresses the strange changeableness of his image. For Julian this altering in the colour of the vernicle reflects a shifting in the appearance of the face of Christ, both in his life and in her revelation. Jesus' face does not remain static, so in his life she muses that Jesus must have looked very fair, the fairest of all (words from Psalm 45:2), up until the sore trials of his Passion, when 'his fair colour was changed with travail and sorrow and passion, dying'. She draws a parallel between this change in image brought about by the humiliation of his suffering and the slow changes she sees his body undergo in the eighth revelation, when she witnesses the process of his dying. The face and body of Jesus shifts and changes. Like our bodies, his body undergoes many changes. These changes Julian sees as reflected in the similar shifting of the 'true image of Jesus' captured on the vernicle. The vernicle was a miraculous imprint of a bodily person, but not a static representation of his form, so it echoes and mirrors the changing visage of Jesus, 'sometime more comfortably and lively, and sometime more piteous and deathlike, as it may be seen in the eighth revelation'.

From Julian's perspective, her engagement with the notion of the image and likeness has come to express a new way of understanding the hiddenness and apparent absence of God. The face of Jesus is not covered by the blood of the cross; it is revealed through the suffering of the cross. Here Jesus' likeness to humanity is realised and, as such, the way in which Jesus truly bore the sins of the world on the cross, that we might be reborn in his likeness, the likeness of one who dwells in this mortal flesh, but where even here the Trinity is found to dwell, is revealed and is made a present reality. The cross, therefore, becomes the means by which we die with Christ to this earthly flesh and, like the pure newborn child, rise to our life now hidden in the Trinity.

Seeking and beholding

Chapter 10 moves from the theological explanation of the hiddenness and presence of Christ to its practical implications for the devout soul and concludes with a devotional lesson. The image of Jesus' face on the vernicle is therefore not bright and fixed but dark, hard to see and constantly shifting. This is not a fixed icon that gazes out at us but rather a mysterious presence that cannot be contained or pinned down. The beauty of his face, however, is not obscured by the changeableness of mortal flesh but rather has become part of it, so that in all the seeming blindness and sin of this life we can now see Jesus' face looking out and through it at us. This life is the place of encounter with the face of Jesus. We do not have to wait for the next life for this encounter.

Julian wants us to learn an important lesson: that seeking Jesus is as important as beholding him in all his glory:

> And this vision was a learning to mine understanding that the continual seeking of the soul pleases God very greatly; for it may do no more than seek, suffer and trust, and this is wrought in the soul that hath it by the Holy Ghost; and the clarity of finding is of his special grace when it is his will.

Unlike the tribulation literature of *The Chastising of God's Children*, which builds up the soul through a process of consolation and desolation, Julian does not have such a robust itinerary for her lovers of Christ. Instead of Christ wilfully hiding his presence from us, so that his absence is a desolation, Julian sees the desire of the soul to know and seek God as an honour, even more so than having a deep mystical beholding of his glory. For Julian, to sit in the cloud of unknowing is our given lot in this life, but what makes it beneficial is to constantly look for where his face appears within the shifting cloud formations rather than the sudden parting of the clouds. She writes:

> The seeking with faith, hope and charity pleases our Lord, and the finding pleases the soul and fulfils it with joy. And thus I learned to my understanding that seeking is as good as beholding for the time that he will suffer the soul to be in travail.

For all those who have never had a close personal experience of the presence of God, Julian gives hope and validity to our search for him. This search is not so much like sitting and waiting to see the flash of blue of the kingfisher, as Ann Lewin describes it in her poem 'Watching for the Kingfisher', but more the attuning of our eyes that we may see him in this world. Julian bids us to look and look and look until we behold:

> It is God's will that we seek him to the beholding of him, for by that he shall show us himself of his special grace when he will. And how a soul shall have him in his beholding, he shall teach himself; and that is most worship to him and profit to thyself and most receiveth of meekness and virtues with the grace and leading of the Holy Ghost; for a soul that only fastens him on to God with very trust, either by seeking or by beholding, it is the most worship that he may do to him, as to my sight. These are two workings that may be seen in this vision: that one is seeking and the other is beholding.

Julian sees this process of seeking as the means by which our blinded eyes come to behold. At the root of it, though, is desire and love, the soul's searching for God, and through this desire the soul is made able through grace to come and behold the face of Christ. This gift of seeking is not seen as something specialised or restricted to contemplatives. Instead, she says it is common to all.

The chapter ends with an ordered practical scheme of three ways in which God wishes the seeking soul to behold. From the chaos and confusion of the shifting images of the changing colour of the vision of the cross now comes clarity and clear sightedness:

> The first is that we seek wilfully and eagerly, without sloth, as it may be through his grace, gladly and merrily without unreasonable heaviness and empty sorrow.

In the medieval period, sloth was not seen as laziness but more akin to the spiritual vice of *apatheia*, or apathy, and in particular religious apathy. There is nothing like apathy to kill spiritual desire.

Julian is also aware of the great sense of sorrow for our sins which can weigh the soul down. Both of these turn our eyes from God and make us dwell on ourselves rather than look up and seek the loving face of Jesus:

> The second is that we abide him steadfastly for his love, without grumbling and striving against him, to our lives' end, for it shall last but awhile.

Drawing on the indwelling nature of Jesus and ourselves from John's gospel, Julian reminds us where we are rooted and grounded, namely in the presence of Christ. Grumbling was the great sin St Benedict warned his community of, for it fragments relationships as the person grumbling asserts their feelings and rights over the community. Grumbling is the destroyer of our relationship with God and our interdependency on Jesus, as we no longer recognise Jesus as Lord ourselves. Only humility and knowledge of his steadfast love can overcome these most human of failings.

Finally, the third is perhaps the hardest:

> That we trust in him mightily with steadfast faith, for it is his will.

In these three things Julian gives the seeking soul ways to pierce its blindness and behold God in its mortal life. These are the things the soul can do to attune its eyes to behold the face of Jesus in this mortal flesh: to search, abide and trust. They are the guide for the humble soul who waits patiently for the day when the Lord:

> shall appear suddenly and blissfully to all his lovers; for his working is secret and he will be perceived and his appearing shall be suddenly swift, and he will be trusted, for he is full courteous and homely – blessed may he be.

Julian closes the chapter with this shout of assurance in the gracious and homely love of God who does not leave us bereft but is closer to us than we are to ourselves. It is this truth that her revelation shows, even in the depth of his perceived absence and withdrawal on the cross. For Julian, Jesus cries out, 'My God, my God, why have you forsaken me?', so that, when we cry out into the silence, we know that even here he is present.

Allow the words of the chapter to linger in your mind.

What thoughts, images and ideas have stood out for you?

What does the face of Jesus look like to you?

Allow your imagination to make Jesus present to you. What would you like to say to him? What does he wish to say to you?

Holding these thoughts and images in your mind, read Julian's words again:

> We know he shall appear suddenly and blissfully to all his lovers; for his working is secret and he will be perceived and his appearing shall be suddenly swift, and he will be trusted, for he is full courteous and homely – blessed may he be.

Laying aside your inner thoughts and feelings, be still in the presence of Jesus.

What will you take away with you from this time of meditation?

Questions to ponder or discuss

- What makes you bored in your life of faith?
- What weighs you down and why?
- What prevents you from trusting in God?
- How would you describe the idea of a holy life to someone else?
- How could you introduce Jesus to someone this week?

Words for the journey

The Lord bless you and keep you;
the Lord make his face to shine upon you, and be gracious to you;
the Lord lift up his countenance upon you, and give you peace.

NUMBERS 6:24–26

*

The fourth revelation

– 9 –

FLOWING BLOOD

Meditation is focused on the life-giving nature of blood and the sheer generosity of the quantity that Julian sees flowing from Jesus. It is linked with the biblical narrative of the flagellation of Jesus and the symbolism of the Eucharist.

And after this I saw, beholding, the body plenteously bleeding in seeming of the scourging, as thus: the fair skin was broken full deep into the tender flesh with sharp smiting all about the sweet body; so plenteously the hot blood ran out that there was seen neither skin nor wound, but as it were all blood.
Revelations of Divine Love, ch. 12

In the fourth revelation Julian returns once more to the foot of the cross. This time her focus homes in on another aspect of the Passion, the bleeding of Christ's body. It seems that we have gone back in time from the third revelation, when Julian drew our gaze to the face of Jesus on the cross, to the scourging of Christ by the soldiers. Yet this revelation, like the others centred on the cross, does not so much follow the sequential narrative of the Passion but rather opens up and lingers on one specific aspect. That does not mean to say that the revelations are not linked to each other; they flow into each other, picking up details, expanding themes and developing thoughts like a meditation on a moving image. In this fourth revelation, we have the development of the image of blood.

Blood has been a theme running through all the revelations so far. In the first, red blood trickled down from under the garland of thorns, which transmuted into great drops that fell like rain from the eaves in their plenteousness. In the second revelation, Jesus' fair face slowly disappeared behind a curtain of drying blood and we saw the bloodied imprint of his face upon the vernicle. Now, in revelation four, the focus returns to the plenteous bleeding of Christ, this time caused not by the crown of thorns but by the scourging of the soldiers. We move from Christ's head to Christ's body.

Flagellation

Right at the beginning, the fourth revelation is associated with the scourging of Jesus. As in the second revelation, however, this scriptural basis is mentioned merely as a point of reference, and the vision quickly moves to focus on the effect it has on Jesus' flesh. The rest of the revelation freely draws on images and statements throughout the late-medieval devotional climate to explore and reveal the goodness of God within this showing. The description of the scourging in the gospels is equally brief, coming after Jesus has been questioned by Pilate. Mark simply says, 'After flogging Jesus, he [Pilate] handed him over to be crucified' (Mark 15:15). Matthew retains the same phrase and John records that 'Pilate took Jesus and had him flogged' (John 19:1). Luke differs slightly in that Pilate offers to have Jesus flogged instead of crucified, but it is the crowd who demands his death. Only Luke excludes any account of Jesus being flogged or scourged. For these two gospel writers, Jesus is first flogged by order of Pilate then handed over to the soldiers to be mocked.

The reason for this detail is that flagellation, or scourging, was a particular Roman form of torture. Hence it is the Roman governor, Pilate, who decrees it. It was an especially horrible form of beating, which sought to render the criminal to a pitiable state of mutilation and suffering, but was not meant to cause death. That is not to say that some did not die as a result of flogging, but death was not the primary aim. The flogging was carried out using a whip that often was tipped with metal barbs. Mel Gibson's film *The Passion of the Christ* sought to give a realistic rendering of the horror of this sentence, and it expresses a similar medieval fascination with the physical horror of the scourging.

The scourging of Christ was a focus of much art and devotional writing in Julian's day, as the devout soul was invited to imaginatively and affectively recreate the moment with their inner eye. This meditative engagement with the suffering of Jesus at the moment of his flogging was not in order to indulge some macabre fascination for torture. There was not the sensationalism of the later Gothic novel, designed to send thrills of fear down the spine at gruesome descriptions of mutilation. Rather the medieval devotional art and literature depicting Christ's suffering sought to elicit a response of love and compassion, which was seen as the proper response to Christ's demonstration of his love on the cross.

It was only later, in the 20th century, in the cross theology of the likes of Jürgen Moltmann and Dietrich Bonhoeffer, that the unity of Christ with all who suffer was fully articulated. For the medieval person, suffering was a daily occurrence, as was the sight of blood, wounds and death. Julian herself lived through two epidemics of the plague, which wiped out a third of the population in 1348 and then again in 1361. Pain was something to be borne, a symptom of this wretched world. Jesus was an icon of this patient suffering, but his human experience was also seen as a gateway, a shared experience that brought Christ into direct encounter with those who loved him. This can be clearly seen in the image of the flagellation in the Holkham Bible Picture Book (Plate 13), dating to the early 14th century, which shows Jesus tied to a tree stump, blood dripping from his body and covered in welt marks from the lashing. Yet his face looks calm, if not sad, and patient under the blows. To suffer with and for Christ was the ultimate demonstration of love by the devout for their suffering Lord.

The medieval mystics of England did not express a solidarity with

Christ's suffering in such an extreme way as their continental sisters did, where we read of brutal acts of harsh asceticism and violent mortification from the likes of the 13th-century Flemish nun Beatrice of Nazareth. Neither did the rapidly growing movement of flagellants, who practised an extreme form of public penance, seem to catch on in England. Instead, the *Ancrene Wisse* famously advises caution in all mortification of the flesh:

> Let no one belt herself with any kind of belt next to the body, except with her confessor's leave, nor wear any iron or hair, or hedgehog skins; let her not beat herself with them, nor with a leaded scourge, with holly briars, nor draw blood from herself without her confessor's leave; let her not sting herself with nettles anywhere, nor beat herself in front, nor cut herself, nor impose on herself too many severe disciplines to quench temptations at one time.

Instead, it was through imagination and meditation that the devout sought a deeper association with Christ in his suffering to evoke compassion and love.

There were numerous devotional writings that lingered on the mutilation of the flagellation to enable them to do this. *The Privity of the Passion*, a 14th-century translation of *Meditationes Vitae Christi*, erroneously attributed to Bonaventure, is a good example of one such meditation on the flogging:

> He stood naked before them, a fair young man, modest in body and beautiful in form beyond all earthly men; he endured the hard, painful beating of his tenderest and purest flesh by these wicked men. The flower of all flesh and of all mankind is now full of dark scars and bloody bruises; on every side the king of heaven's blood streams down from every part of his blessed body. He was beaten and beaten again, blister upon blister, and wound upon wound, until both the beaters and the spectators were weary, and then they unbound him.

There are a number of ways in which Julian's vision resonates with this standard form of meditation on the scourging. But there are also some significant differences.

In a single sentence Julian articulates her vision in language and images that would have had deep associations within the medieval mind:

> The fair skin was broken full deep into the tender flesh with sharp smiting all about the sweet body;

In both cases, there is an emphasis on the 'fair', 'tender' and 'sweet' flesh of Jesus, with both texts using these very words. As we saw with the fair face of Jesus in the second revelation, his appearance was thought to reflect the words of Psalm 45:

> You are the most handsome of men; grace is poured upon your lips; therefore God has blessed you forever.
>
> PSALM 45:2

Both Julian and the author of the *Privity* bring this understanding to the fore and contrast it with the deep wounding Christ's body receives. Julian uses greater economy in her language, which brings a force to her writing, but both express the same depth of feeling at imagining the tender, sweet flesh of Christ being rent with deep and smiting wounds.

While Julian draws upon the language and imagery of her cultural heritage to describe her vision, there are also a number of ways in which she alters and expands it into new ways of thinking. First, and perhaps most obvious, unlike the *Privity* and the image of the flagellation in the Holkham Bible Picture Book, Julian's revelation makes no mention of those who carried out the flagellation. Much like the roof boss in Norwich Cathedral, which depicts only disembodied hands mocking Christ, so in Julian's revelation the soldiers or wicked men are nameless and there is no sense that they are held in any blame for their actions. This may be a precursor of our modern awareness of endemic anti-Semitism, but it is more likely linked with the 'foul, black covering' of the second revelation, where Jesus is depicted as taking on the sin of humanity in general rather than the actions of individuals in particular. Second, while the *Privity* mentions the blood streaming down from Jesus' side, Julian lingers on this detail and expands it in quantity until neither skin nor wounds can be seen and all is blood.

All blood

One of the disconcerting aspects of the late-medieval period to a modern audience is the way images and descriptions of the cross simply drip with blood. In the late-medieval German image of the crucifixion from the Schnütgen Museum in Cologne (see Plate 14), Jesus' blood rains down in great spurts upon the saints, who grip hold of his cross, while the figure of Jesus himself has become subsumed until he has become literally all blood. The image encapsulates an incongruity within late-medieval devotion to the blood of Christ: the sense in which Jesus' blood is shed through a violent rending of his flesh through flagellation and at the same time the life-giving qualities of that blood, which not only connected the devout to their Saviour by its sacrificial shedding but also washed them.

This is an idea and motif summed up in the iconography of the pelican. Medieval bestiaries, which explained the natural world in relation to the story of salvation, saw young pelicans' striking their mother's face until she bled as an image of sin. Enraged by such ingratitude for her loving devotion, the mother bird would kill her young, only to revive them after three days by piercing her own side and letting her blood fall upon them. It was therefore an image closely associated with the shedding of Christ's blood on the cross and can be found on the frame of the Despenser Retable at Norwich Cathedral. In a similar way, Julian's controlled description of her vision of the scourging of Jesus breaks out in somewhat surreal terms as she moves from considering the welts on his flesh to the blood that gushed forth:

> So plenteously the hot blood ran out that there was seen neither skin nor wound, but as it were all blood. And when it came to where it should fall down, then it vanished; notwithstanding, the bleeding continued a while till it might be seen with consideration.

In this description we see not only a connection and development of Julian's second revelation around the motif of blood but also its relation to the language and ideas of late-medieval devotional culture.

Hot blood

In Julian's first revelation her focus is drawn to consider in detail the blood which trickled down from under the crown of thorns. One aspect of these great drops of blood was the way they emerged from Christ's veins as pellets:

> In the coming out it was brown red, for the blood was full thick; and in the spreading abroad it was bright red; and when it came to the brows it vanished.

As we have seen, this contemplation of the way blood oozes from a wound is both realistic and visceral, making the events of the Passion very real and immediate. But there is also a strange incongruity in Julian's description, for it reverses the usual way blood changes colour. Blood usually emerges from a wound as bright red and then, as it coagulates, becomes red brown and thick, but in Julian's description of her vision it is the other way round. Rather than dismissing this as a misapprehension on Julian's part, or writing it off as a visionary error, it has in fact a deep theological significance that becomes clearer in the fourth revelation.

It's a detail that can easily be passed over, but the manner in which Julian describes the blood flowing from Jesus' wounds as being hot in fact leaps off the page. This blood is not dead and dried, separated from the body of Jesus, but rather is full of life; it is his lifeblood, which he is imparting to the world. So the blood is bright red, hot and freshly poured out so that it may bring life to those who receive it through the Eucharistic cup. Perhaps more than the body of Christ, it was the blood of Christ that was intimately and powerfully connected with the Passion in the medieval mind. The cup of Christ, which was only received at high festivals, was a tangible incorporation of the faithful with the actual person of Jesus. For his blood was seen, in the Eucharistic offering, as recalling something given in the past but also as a continual act of self-giving by Christ, which united those who drank his blood in a deep, incorporating way.

Precious plenty

The other aspect of the first revelation that is developed and deepened here in the fourth revelation is that of the plenteous nature of Christ's blood:

> And this was so plenteous to my sight that methought, if it had been so in nature and in substance for that time, it should have made the bed all blood and passed over and about it. And then came to my mind that God has made waters plenteous in earth to our service and to our bodily ease, for tender love that he has to us, but yet likens it better that we take full homely his blessed blood to wash us of sin; for there is no liquor that is made which he likes so well to give us; for it is most plenteous as it is most precious, and that by the virtue of his blessed Godhead.

Whereas in the first revelation Julian rooted the plenteous nature of the blood of Christ within the daily domestic life of her reader, here her reflections are more theological and soteriological.

As Julian sees the fresh, hot blood pour from Christ's wounds, she is reminded of an image from Psalm 65:9: 'You visit the earth and water it, you greatly enrich it; the river of God is full of water.' In the psalm it is water which God pours out to replenish and enable the earth to grow, but for Julian the thing which allows human beings to grow and flourish is the plenteous outpouring of Christ's blood. This may well be an allusion to the waters of baptism, but it is more likely that Julian is referring to the penitential link between Christ's blood and the forgiveness of sins, which is rooted in numerous scriptural passages, not least Jesus' own words of institution at the last supper: 'This is my blood of the covenant, which is poured out for many for the forgiveness of sins' (Matthew 26:28).

During the medieval period there was also a devotional motif which linked both baptism and the forgiveness of sins with the blood of Jesus. In his early 15th-century *Instructions to Parish Priests*, John Mirk expresses this theological link between them when he writes: 'To his bliss us lead that for us on the cross did bleed. *Septem sacramenta ecclesia* [Seven sacraments of the church].' Likewise, in art this link between the seven sacraments and the wounds of Christ was visualised by ribbons of blood flowing from the five wounds in Christ's hands, feet and side, and emanating out to standard representations of the seven sacraments. For instance, in the late-medieval *vulneral* windows of St Michael's Church, Doddiscombsleigh, Devon, a red beam of light connects a later Victorian Christ to each of the seven sacraments. What this iconography clearly depicts is that the saving, life-giving blood of Christ is accessible to all but that this is only available in and through *Ecclesia Mater*, the motherhood of the church or Mother Church, who dispenses the precious drops of Christ's saving blood through the sacraments.

Julian's vision presents a very different notion of the accessibility of Christ's blood. It is not contained within precious droplets, measured out in payments for purgatory, but rather the blood of Christ is seen to flow freely, lavishly and plenteously throughout creation and right into the homely, humble domestic world of ordinary people. In this way Julian develops the domesticity of the water flooding off the eaves and the herring scales in the first revelation with the domestic world of her own chamber. This small space contains her vision and gives it boundaries and borders, and yet, within this ordinary place and time of the present moment, Julian's vision reaches beyond the limitations of the daily, homely world to also express the theological and saving work of Christ, whose blood is shed in lavish and excessive quantities for all.

In a beautiful interplay of the words 'precious' and 'plenty', Julian concludes the chapter by exploring this notion of containment and expansion in three areas that have a very cosmic dimension to their reach. Julian smashes through the restriction of the precious drops of Christ's blood as it breaks out of its sense of containment to descend down to hell, overflow the earth like a second flood and ascend up into heaven, bringing the fourth revelation to an ecstatic end with the overwhelming sense of the sheer lavishness of Christ's love:

> The precious plenty of his dearworthy blood descended into hell and burst her bonds and delivered all that were there who longed for the court of heaven. The precious plenty of his dearworthy blood overflowed all the earth and is ready to wash all creatures of sin who be of good will, have been and shall be. The precious plenty of his dearworthy blood ascended into heaven to the blessed body of our Lord Jesus Christ, and there is in him bleeding and praying for us to the Father – and is and shall be as long as it is needed. And evermore it flows throughout all heaven enjoying the salvation of all mankind who are there and shall be there, fulfilling the number who fell.

Going deeper

Give yourself some time to linger on these words by Julian:

> The precious plenty of his dearworthy blood descended into hell and burst her bonds and delivered all that were there who longed for the court of heaven.
>
> The precious plenty of his dearworthy blood overflowed all the earth and is ready to wash all creatures of sin who be of good will, have been and shall be.
>
> The precious plenty of his dearworthy blood ascended into heaven to the blessed body of our Lord Jesus Christ, and there is in him bleeding and praying for us to the Father – and is and shall be as long as it is needed. And evermore it flows throughout all heaven enjoying the salvation of all mankind who are there and shall be there, fulfilling the number who fell.

What strikes you about her words?

How does this passage make you feel?

What does the blood of Christ mean to you?

Allow your thoughts and feelings to guide you to a place of stillness and gratitude.

What will you take away with you from this time of meditation?

Questions to ponder or discuss

- How do you respond to imaginatively meditating on the wounding of Christ?
- What does the imagery of blood say to you?
- What do you value about the Eucharist?
- How would you explain the Eucharist to someone who has never experienced it?
- How does Christ's suffering affect the way you see the suffering of others?

Words for the journey

> This is my blood of the covenant, which is poured out for many for the forgiveness of sins.
>
> MATTHEW 26:28

*

The eighth revelation

– 10 –

DYING FOR LOVE

This chapter focuses on Julian's descriptions of Jesus' dying on the cross. The meditation is centred on sharing another's sorrow – Jesus' sharing in our sorrows and our sharing in his through love. Based on Jesus' words 'I thirst', the chapter explores Jesus' thirsting and our own, and it comes to marvel on the transformative power of the cross.

After this Christ showed a part of his Passion near to his dying. I saw his sweet face, as it were dry and bloodless with pale dying; and afterwards more pale, dead, languishing and then turned more dead into blue, and afterwards more brown blue, as the flesh turned more deeply dead; for his Passion showed to me properly in his blessed face and namely in his lips; there I saw four colours, that before were fresh, red and attractive to my sight.

Revelations of Divine Love, ch. 16

We have moved on, not only in Julian's text, but also in her vision. In the intervening three showings Julian has, first, heard words of reassurance within her soul that through Jesus' cross the devil is overcome; second, her understanding has been taken up into the heavenly courts, where she has seen the worshipful gratitude that the Lord has for his servants; and finally, she has experienced in a spiritual way the oscillating states of *wele* and *woe*. Now, in the eighth revelation, Julian's vision returns us again to stand at the foot of the cross.

As with her other revelations of the cross, there is a sense of continuum between this showing and the ones which have gone before. After watching the blood drain out of Christ's body, Julian returns once more to focus on Jesus' face. But now the time frame has changed, and she sees the last piteous pains of Christ's death played out in the 'often changing of colour' of his face. This is a hard read and a passage that is not often used on study or quiet days on Julian.

One of the reasons it is so hard to read is the way Julian lingers on the detail of her vision with minute and exact precision. Even if you wanted to skip over this harrowing description of dying, Julian simply won't let you. She wants you to see and feel every element. So her words continue with unremitting exactitude:

> This was a sorrowful change to see in this deep dying, and also the nose shrivelled and dried, to my sight, and the sweet body was brown and black, all turned out of the fair lively colour of himself into dry dying; for at the same time that our Lord and blessed Saviour died upon the cross there was a dry, keen wind and was cold, as to my sight; and what time the precious blood was bled out of the sweet body that might pass therefrom, there yet dwelled a moisture in the sweet flesh of Christ, as it was shown.

It seems that this is half the purpose of the text. Julian wants to enable her reader not just to objectively read about someone else's vision in a disconnected and dispassionate way, but also to be drawn into a place of discomfort, suffering even, where we feel in every sense the agony of sitting at the foot of the cross and watching Christ die. Unlike her affective devotional counterparts Julian does not use highly emotive language to do this. She is not gushing forth tears or making passionate declarations of love or longing like Margery Kempe. Instead, she simply describes what she is shown. Julian looks and looks and looks, until she beholds, and then uses words in a measured and forensic way to help her reader to re-image her vision in their own mind and feel the dying of Christ in their own hearts.

While on first reading Julian's words seem to tumble out as if they were written at the very moment Julian was witnessing her vision, there is a structure and progression behind her composition. She clearly focuses the description of her vision on the face of Jesus – his skin, lips and nose – linking us back to the second revelation. From that vision Julian picks up the detail of his face as changing in colour, and here, in this eighth revelation, she explores and lingers on the various colours that shifted and altered through her vision. She even systematises the colours into a list for us and uses contrast to highlight the difference between the dying Christ and his sweet, fair and lively face.

A colour that was often used in lyrics and meditations on the Passion during the medieval period was blue. Richard Rolle follows a general devotional trend in describing the dying flesh of Christ:

> The flesh, where the cross sits, is all made raw; the blains and the blisters are livid and blue.

In a way this is a trope of the Passion meditation tradition, just as Christ's robes are invariably depicted as blue in iconography to denote his divine nature. But the colour blue was also associated with bruising and more importantly with the cleansing of sin. In the Vulgate Bible, which was used during the medieval period, Proverbs 20:30 reads differently to our modern renderings as:

> The blueness of a wound shall wipe away evils and stripes in the more inwards parts of the body.

To the medieval mind, the very colour of Christ's wounds were a visual motif of the fact that the wounds of Jesus took away the sin of the world.

The reality of death

Yet lying behind the devotional motifs and textual composition, there is also a sense in this passage that Julian is not just describing a vision of the dying of Christ but also giving a first-hand account of the experience of watching someone die before her very eyes.

We know very little of Julian the person. There is scant, if any, external documentary evidence, and her texts give little more away. Of the scarce details we do know, there is one crucial clue: Julian tells us that she had her revelation in 1373, when she was 30 years old. This would have meant that she was born in 1343 and therefore lived through the great pandemic of the 14th century and its subsequent recurrences. The first wave of the plague or Black Death struck England in 1348 and quickly spread throughout the country. In Norwich alone, 12,000 people died during the two years it raged across the country, when 30–45% of the entire population was wiped out. Julian would only have been a young girl at the time. However, when the second wave struck, in 1361–64, Julian would have been around 20 years old and still only 25 when the plague returned yet again in 1368. These later recurrences particularly took their toll on young men and children. Julian therefore lived through a devastating period when death swept through the population in the most painful and prolonged way. It is therefore extremely likely that Julian would have known and experienced something of the plague, if not first-hand, then at least by report.

The theologian Benedicta Ward has suggested that Julian not only knew about the Black Death but indeed also had first-hand experience of its terrifying effects. It has been argued that, before she entered the anchorhold, Julian was not a nun, as many artistic representations depict her, but in fact had her own home and family who died as a result of the plague. If this theory is correct, it would mean Julian watched her husband and children slowly succumb to the effects of the plague. Julian possibly knew what it was to sit and watch a loved one die in the most harrowing of circumstances.

While this is purely speculative and based upon textual hints and suggestions, there are elements of her description of the dying of Jesus that resonate with the effects of the plague.

One of the most famous medieval accounts of the plague is found in Boccaccio's *The Decameron* of 1353, which tells of a group of nobles who escape the city of Florence, which is ravaged by plague. He writes:

> In men and women alike it first betrayed itself by the emergence of certain tumours in the groin or armpits, some of which grew as large as a common apple, others as an egg... From the two said parts of the body this deadly *gavocciolo* soon began to propagate and spread itself in all directions indifferently; after which the form of the malady began to change, black spots or livid making their appearance in many cases on the arm or the thigh or elsewhere, now few and large, now minute and numerous. As the *gavocciolo* had been and still was an infallible token of approaching death, such also were these spots on whomsoever they showed themselves.

The hallmark of bubonic plague is the *gavocciolo* or boils, which surface in the armpits and groin but soon spread across the body. This is accompanied by vomiting blood and lesions on the skin that are black and livid. Bubonic plague also causes gangrene, which slowly turns the body black as the flesh literally dies on the bone – another colour, along with blue, which marked the slow dying of Christ in Julian's vision.

Though it is much later than the time of Julian, the 1515 Isenheim Altarpiece by Matthias Grünewald (see Plate 15) not only visually captures the wasting body of plague sufferers but also resonates with the horror of Julian's description of the dying Jesus. Commissioned by the monks of the Monastery of St Anthony in Issenheim in north-eastern France, who cared for those who suffered from the plague and various skin diseases, it shows the dying Christ covered with plague sores and lesions. His head is hanging down and his mouth falls open with lips parched in the last throes of death. This is a harrowing image of suffering, much like Julian's words; both are painful to consider. But for the sufferers of the plague who were laid in front of this image, it spoke of a God who suffered with them and for them. Whether Julian's eighth revelation was shaped and articulated through her first-hand experience of death from the plague we cannot say for certain, but this image helps to bring her words alive for us in all their lingering pain and suffering.

The long night

Time worked in a strange way in Julian's vision. Sometimes it sped up, as in the actions of the soldiers, and sometimes it slowed right down. Invariably, Julian's writing reflects this expansion and contraction of the measured process of time within her vision. Like her vision, Julian's writing enables her to hold the historical moment of the Passion within the eternal present. But, much like when a film is paused, fast-forwarded and rewound, her words also enable the events of the Passion to be paused and contemplated in detail, fast-forwarded to a seminal moment or rewound to focus on a past detail. In this way Julian's writing captures the lingering but also dislocating nature of her vision. She tries to help us by systematising what she saw and repeating certain details, expanding on them to give clarity and meaning. However, her writing still rests on an experience which she is remembering in her past and bringing to our present reality.

Already we have had a sense from her text that Julian's vision lingered in a harrowing way upon the details of Christ's dying, and her descriptive and detailed words have similarly held us in a place of discomfort. Now she gives us some sense of how long this process of dying took:

> And though this pain was bitter and sharp, it was full long lasting, as to my sight, and painfully dried up all the lively spirit

> of Christ's flesh. Thus, I saw the sweet flesh die, in seeming by one part after another part, drying with marvellous pains. And as long as any spirit had life in Christ's flesh, so long he suffered pain. This long pain seemed to me as if he had been dead seven nights, dying, at the point of passing away, suffering the last pain. And when I said it seemed to me as if had been seven nights dead, it means that the sweet body was so discoloured, so dry, so shrivelled, so deathly and so piteous as if he had been dead for seven nights, continually dying. And methought the dying of Christ's flesh was the most pain, and the last, of his Passion.

It is as if the process of writing enables Julian to realise and understand more fully what she sees. As she looked on the vision of Christ's dying and now writes about it, Julian comes to realise that her vision is showing the pains and suffering of someone who has suffered not for three hours on the cross but rather for seven days. A whole week's pain and slow dying of the flesh has been contracted into a single moment in her vision.

The meaning of seven nights does not originate from the gospel story, but it has great significance to Julian's own story, for this was the number of days that she herself had lain dying. In chapter 3 of her *Revelations of Divine Love*, Julian carefully records the process of her illness:

> And when I was thirty and a half years old, God sent me a bodily sickness in which I lay three days and three nights, and on the fourth night I took all my rites of holy church and believed not to live till day. And after this I languished for two days and two nights and on the third night, I believed that I had passed away, and so it seemed to those who were there.

Julian goes on to describe how her own illness felt like a gradual dying as her body felt dead from the middle down and her pain so acute that she thought she would die. As she looks at Christ on the cross, she sees her own pain and dying reflected in not only Christ's dying and agony but actually the way in which he has taken that dying on himself.

The double thirst

As Julian ponders her vision of the death of Christ, his words 'I thirst' come to her mind. These are the fifth of what has come to be known as the seven last words of the cross. They come at the end point of Jesus' death on the cross and are only recorded in John's gospel. There is a sense in this gospel that Jesus goes to the cross in full charge of the situation. His words and actions are deliberate, and in a number of places John recounts how they specifically fulfil previous scripture. The same is the case here:

> After this, when Jesus knew that all was now finished, he said (in order to fulfil the scripture), 'I am thirsty.' A jar full of sour wine was standing there. So they put a sponge full of the wine on a branch of hyssop and held it to his mouth. When Jesus had received the wine, he said, 'It is finished.' Then he bowed his head and gave up his spirit.
>
> JOHN 19:28–30

From earliest times Jesus' thirst was interpreted as a 'double thirst', as Julian likewise describes it. First, the external physical or bodily parching and drying out of Jesus' body as he hung upon the cross, making him cry out for relief. Second, the spiritual or ghostly yearning of the soul for God from the psalms, which Jesus is fulfilling:

> O God, you are my God, I seek you, my soul thirsts for you; my flesh faints for you, as in a dry and weary land where there is no water.
>
> PSALM 63:1

> I stretch out my hands to you; my soul thirsts for you like a parched land.
> PSALM 143:6

This notion of a double meaning was widely disseminated in medieval devotional literature. In the *Ancrene Wisse*, Christ's thirst is 'nothing but desire for the salvation of our souls', while Richard Rolle, in his *Meditations on the Passion*, expresses the widespread medieval devotional understanding when he writes: 'But, sweet Jesus, this thirst was manifold: in body for pain, and in soul thou thirsted deliverance of souls in hell that here in life had kept thy laws.' Julian divides these two aspects and considers them in turn; the bodily thirst in chapter 17 and the ghostly thirst in chapter 31. We will just consider the former.

The bodily thirst

If you felt that the first description of Christ's death in chapter 16 was difficult to read, you will find that Julian ratchets up the horror in an extraordinary way in chapter 17, for even the little moisture that was left in his body now drains away, leaving a dead, lifeless rag of skin flapping on a piece of wood. Once again, her vision is picking up and developing an image from a previous aspect of the revelation. Julian has previously focused on the face of Christ; now she considers the loss of enormous quantities of blood, as she did in the fourth revelation. But where this revelation differs is that, whereas previously Jesus' Passion was seen as life-giving and eucharistic, now the true extent of the costliness of that self-giving by Christ on the cross is realised in all its enormity:

> The blessed body dried alone for a long time, with twisting of the nails and weight of the body; for I understood that for tenderness of the sweet hands and of the sweet feet, by the greatness, hardness and grievousness of the nails, the wounds waxed wider and the body sagged because of the weight by

> hanging for a long time; and the piercing and twisting of the head and binding of the crown, all baked with dried blood, with the sweet hair clinging, with the dry flesh, to the thorns and the thorns to the dying flesh... And furthermore I saw that the sweet skin and tender flesh, with the hair and blood, was all raised and loose above from the bone with the thorns where through it was pierced on many pieces, as a cloth that sags, as it would hastily have fallen for its heaviness and loss because of its natural moisture.

Once again Julian's description of her vision resonates with the imagery of Grünewald's painting of the crucifixion on the Isenheim Altarpiece (see Plate 16). This detail captures Julian's description of the slow hanging weight of the body of Christ, which bears downs on the nails, distorting the foot and causing the wounds they form to open still wider. In a twist of irony, the life-giving moisture or water of the cross, which Christ pours out through his blood, now becomes another weight which drags Christ's body down until it becomes nothing but a cloth flaying in the wind. How different is this pitiful and horrendous image to that of the beautiful language of the clothing of love, which we are enfolded within like children, in chapter 5. We have moved away from the lovely, sweet, soft language of love, which is so often associated with Julian, and entered a visionary world which truly grasps and names the cost of that love. For we cannot forget that while we linger on this slow death of Jesus, we are in fact contemplating another clothing, the foul black covering of sin from the second revelation. What we look at is the dying of Christ, but what we behold is the consequence of sin.

You may be beginning to wonder why on earth you are reading Julian, given that her writing is so harrowing and grotesque! This seems to have little to do with building up the body of Christ, but rather shredding it through grim descriptions of sin. But all becomes clearer as we reach the end of chapter 17. Her description of the dying of Christ continues many lines beyond those quoted above, returning to the garland of thorns, which now is soaked in blood.

Julian sees another garland formed by the dried flesh which sags around the crown, forming a garland upon a garland. His face, too, which was once so sweet and fair, is now like a board, wrinkled, small and burnt brown. Both of these annihilate the positive image of the garland in the first revelation and the sweet face, hidden behind a veil, of the second revelation. It is as if Julian can bear it no more, for the 'showing of Christ's pains filled me full of pain'. For a moment Julian completely forgets about her own illness and suffering and is caught up in the horror of the pain of Christ. Now she repents that she had ever asked to see a vision of the Passion and to share in Christ's suffering as she had so piously requested. Now she realises what that actually means.

It means to see and know the worst pain and suffering there ever was or will be. She asks, 'Is any pain like this?', and the response she is given in her reason is:

> 'Hell is another pain, for there is despair. But of all the pain that leads to salvation, this is the most pain: to see thy love suffer.' How might any pain be more to me than to see him that is all my life, all my bliss and all my joy suffer?

Suddenly the dawn breaks in Julian's comprehension and her writing. She has put us through the mill, sat us at the foot of the cross and made us behold and live the grim horrors of the suffering of Christ as a consequence of sin. But Julian realises that the reason she suffers so at this vision of the cross is because of how much she cares, indeed loves, the person who is slowly dying before her very eyes. Her text places us in this same space before the cross and through her unremitting descriptive language also brings us to this place of realisation that our agony is as a result of our love for Christ:

> How might any pain be more to me than to see him that is all my life, all my bliss and all my joy suffer? Here felt I truly that I loved Christ so much above myself that there was no pain that might be suffered like to that sorrow that I had to see him in pain.

Through her text Julian has brought us to that place of noughting, where we are invited, like her, to die to ourselves for love. So the revelation of the cross has turned from being an experience of suffering to a realisation of love.

If you feel able to, sit with Julian at the foot of the cross in all its discomfort.

> And furthermore I saw that the sweet skin and tender flesh, with the hair and blood, was all raised and loose above from the bone with the thorns where through it was pierced on many pieces, as a cloth that sags, as it would hastily have fallen for its heaviness and loss because of its natural moisture.

- How does Julian's description make you feel?
- How do you imagine the cross of Christ?
- How do you respond to Christ's act of love?

Acknowledging your inner thoughts and feelings, allow them to focus your mind and heart on the person of Christ.

What will you take away with you from this time of meditation?

Questions to ponder or discuss

- How do you personally relate to the suffering of Jesus?
- Why did Jesus have to suffer?
- Why does God allow suffering to continue?
- How would you explain to someone why Good Friday is good?
- How can you bring love and life to someone who is suffering this week?

Words for the journey

> For God so loved the world that he gave his only Son, so that everyone who believes in him may not perish but may have eternal life.
>
> JOHN 3:16

*

The ninth revelation

– 11 –

THE THREE HEAVENS

Picking up on the transformative power of the cross, this chapter is based on Julian's description of three heavens and is linked to Jesus' words 'Today you will be with me in Paradise.' The nature of paradise is explored, along with Julian's Trinitarian notion of three heavens where we are crowned. Linking back to the crown of thorns of the first chapter, this new heavenly crown and what it might mean is unfolded.

> Then said our good Lord Jesus Christ: 'Are you well pleased that I suffered for you?' I said: 'Yes, good Lord, gramercy. Yes, good Lord, blessed may you be!' Then said Jesus, our kind Lord: 'If you are pleased, I am pleased. It is a joy, a bliss, an endless pleasure to me that I ever suffered the Passion for you; and if I might suffer more, I would suffer more.' In this feeling my understanding was lifted up into heaven, and there I saw three heavens, of which sight I greatly marvelled.
>
> *Revelations of Divine Love*, ch. 22

With the ninth revelation the mood has changed dramatically, as if the dark night has passed and the dawn has come. No longer do we have horrific descriptions of bodily suffering and anguish but rather an expression of Christ's love and devotion. But this is not a simple transition from dark to light, cross to resurrection. Julian has sat at the foot of the cross, in all its pain and horror, until she is able to make this remarkable statement in chapter 19, that she:

> Learnt to choose Jesus as my heaven, whom I saw only in pain at that time.

Heaven, for Julian, is not a future world of peace, comfort and escapism, not simply a state of being after death where 'all shall be well'; rather it is a person, the person of Christ on the cross. If you want to know what heaven looks like, then look at Christ on the cross. How on earth can Julian say this? Before we can move on to the three heavens, we must linger a little longer with Julian at the foot of the cross and try to comprehend what she means by these extraordinary words. Julian's thinking is dense and complex, but also profound and worth taking a little time to understand, because it gives a deeper sense of joy and love for the person of Christ.

A lesson of love

Chapters 18–21, which separate Julian's description of her eighth and ninth revelations, act as a bridging device, a lesson that moves the reader from the crippling agony of watching the suffering of Jesus on the cross to a sense of delight in the bliss of heaven which Christ has made possible through his cross. The previous revelation concluded with Julian realising that the agony she felt from standing at the foot of the cross resulted not so much from what she was observing but from her own love and devotion for the one who suffered. This love for Christ made Julian forget her own suffering, drew her out of herself and caused her to be filled with enormous compassion, and experience a pain for her beloved that surpassed all others. In the following chapter, Julian concludes, from her own feelings, that this is just a small part of how Mary, who loved Christ more than all others, must have felt at the foot of the cross, and so it is for all his disciples and 'true lovers'. From her youth, Julian had wished to stand at the foot of the cross with all Christ's lovers and know the full extent of Christ's bodily suffering. Now she has experienced this to some degree and placed us in the same sphere of knowledge and experience through the words of her text.

As a result, Julian realises that there is 'a great oneing [unity/oneness] between Christ and us', which means that when he was in pain, we were in pain. Just as the sky went black and the sun was seen no more, the earth shook and all creatures that could suffer pain did so at the hour of his death, so we, whether blessed or cursed, feel and share in the death of Christ on the cross. In a way this is a reversal of the idea that, on the cross, it is Christ who shares in our suffering, takes on our pain. Where Julian had seen Christ dying for the same period of time as her own illness, so taking on himself her own individual pain, now through her experience of agony at seeing his suffering she realises that when Christ suffers, because of his oneness with humanity it is us who also share in his pain and suffering:

> Thus was our Lord Jesus noughted for us, and we stand all in this manner noughted with him.

So when a friendly voice tells her to 'look up to heaven to his Father', Julian refuses, thinking perhaps that this is a voice to tempt her away from Christ. Instead, she chooses to sit at the foot of the cross, in all its pain and agony, for here Julian knows she is one with Christ, a true lover who trusts in him alone.

Even as Julian chooses to look upon the wooden crucifix and remain in this place of suffering, love and longing, suddenly she sees, in the same cross, Christ's face change into blissful cheer, which correspondingly changes her own. Time for Julian has collapsed into an eternal moment on the cross, which is both a single instant and eternal, and the place where Christ suffers in and for humanity is at the same time also the place where his resurrection love and joy are seen and known. In this way, she radically brings the resurrection right on to the cross, closing down any sense that sequential, linear suffering is followed by joy – first pain and then all will be well. It is no wonder that she chooses Jesus on the cross for her heaven, for:

> I understood that we be now, in our Lord's meaning, in his cross with him in our pains and our passion, dying, and we wilfully

> abide in the same cross with his help and his grace up to the last point, suddenly he shall change his cheer to us, and we shall be with him in heaven.

Between the one and the other there is no time at all. Once we see and know what bliss this is, Julian states, we will not worry or be aggrieved by the pain we now suffer. It is our blindness and foolishness to this truth that causes us to linger on our own wounds and sins, picking over them, reopening them, playing back the sins of the past over and over in our heads. Likewise we linger on Christ's pain and Passion, but Christ suffers in, with and for all humanity, so that even at the point of most despair and suffering he may bring us to the utmost bliss.

Are you well pleased?

Julian's text has beautifully led us through this lesson of love to the ninth revelation, which she describes in terms of 'the infinite love of Christ'. The first part of this showing is a remarkable dialogue between Jesus and Julian. We can only assume that Christ addresses Julian from the cross, but it is now out of his blessed cheer of joy that he speaks to her and says, 'Are you well pleased that I suffered for you?'

In the middle English of her original writing, Julian expresses the question with the word *payd*. This can be translated in one of two ways. First, as 'pleased', as I have done above, which expresses a tender, intimate relationship of love and resonates with the words of the Father to the Son at the moment he rises from the waters of baptism. As the Spirit of God descends on Jesus a voice from heaven is heard saying, 'You are my Son, the Beloved; with you I am well pleased' (Luke 3:22). In Julian's revelation, it is Jesus, the second person of the Trinity, who asks Julian if she is 'well pleased' at all he has done on the cross, like a lover seeking reassurance from the beloved for an act of love. Throughout medieval art and literature, the act of salvation was often expressed in the terms and imagery of courtly love, where Christ the lover knight sought to joust with the devil to free his lady the soul. It is in these terms that the *Ancrene Wisse* sought to persuade those who were enclosed to respond with love to their lover knight. Likewise Julian is addressed by Christ in similar courteous terms of loving devotion, but the tone of his words to Julian far surpasses those of the formal lover knight. Instead, we hear the Lord of heaven and earth, who enfolded Julian in his love, now asking her in the most vulnerable and heart-rending terms whether she is happy because of his act of love on the cross.

Second, the word *payd* can also be translated as 'satisfied', a term which still has deep theological significance today. The satisfaction theory is perhaps most widely known and succinctly summed up in the lines from that popular Good Friday hymn 'There is a green hill far away':

> *There was no other good enough to pay the price of sin*
> *He only could unlock the gate of heaven and let us in.*

Developed by Anselm in the 12th century and built upon by Aquinas in the 13th, the satisfaction theory understood the theology of the cross in terms of the penitential system of the church, in addition to the feudal law of the time. Put simply, sin is an offence to God and God's justice; but humanity, who are steeped in sin, are unable to offer the necessary satisfaction or reparation for their offence. Only Christ, a God/man, one who is without sin and yet fully human, could make reparation for the offence of sin. Here in her ninth vision, Christ asks Julian, 'Are you well satisfied that I died for you?' These words are not spoken to the Father, the one who is aggrieved and thwarted by sin, but rather to the human soul, the one who has suffered the consequences of sin. Thus, Julian comes to realise that the cross is not so much about inflicting pain and punishment to pay the dues of sin, nor is it solely about Christ receiving the humiliation we rightly deserve; it is about something greater – it is about forgiveness and reconciliation. These do not come after the dark night in the dawn of a new day, the third day, but are found only within and through the events of Good Friday.

Julian's response to these words by Christ captures not only a reciprocal love and devotion, but also a moment of insight and awe, which flows out in a spontaneous expression of wonder and praise: 'Yes, good Lord, gramercy. Yes, good Lord, blessed may you be!' The terrible suffering of the cross has not so much been transformed into an act of devotion and love by Christ, but rather Julian sees within the bodily suffering the ghostly sense and meaning of the Passion. She has moved from seeing bodily to beholding spiritually. So Jesus' reply to Julian reminds us of the ghostly presence of the whole Trinity at the Passion:

> If you are satisfied, I am satisfied. It is a joy, a bliss, an endless pleasure to me that I ever suffered the Passion for you; and if I might suffer more, I would suffer more.

What a truly remarkable insight into the theology of the cross. So often we wish to hasten on Good Friday, bearing with the lamentations and bleak churches until they can be decked with garlands of flowers ready for the Easter joy. For Julian the very words of reproach from the Sarum Missal for Good Friday, when Christ calls from the cross, 'What more should I do for you and have not done?', echoing the words of Isaiah 5:4, are spoken now out of sheer love for sinful, foolish humanity, who are incapable of seeing beyond the pain, humiliation and agony of this mortal life to the presence of God's redeeming love within.

The three heavens

Through the trio of words, 'joy', 'bliss' and 'endless liking', Julian's understanding is suddenly taken up into the second part of her revelation. It is as if the clouds have parted and she is taken into a mysterious, inner realm of sight and knowing where she sees three heavens, the three persons of the Trinity. Each of the revelations we have considered in this book have all had some fundamental connection with the gospel story of the Passion. This revelation in turn is rooted in the words of Christ to the thief on the cross who hung alongside him. Just as Christ speaks to Julian, so he tells the penitent thief, 'Today you will be with me in Paradise.'

The account is found only in Luke's gospel, the gospel most concerned with reconciliation of the lost, the outcast and the outsider. Even at his hour of death, Jesus in this gospel is presented as ever seeking to bring those who are lost home. Luke records that as Jesus hangs upon the cross slowly dying:

> One of the criminals who were hanged there kept deriding him and saying, 'Are you not the Messiah? Save yourself and us!' But the other rebuked him, saying, 'Do you not fear God, since you are under the same sentence of condemnation? And we indeed have been condemned justly, for we are getting what we deserve for our deeds, but this man has done nothing wrong.' Then he said, 'Jesus, remember me when you come into your kingdom.' He replied, 'Truly I tell you, today you will be with me in Paradise.'
>
> LUKE 23:39–43

Many a Good Friday address has reflected on these words: who said them, who they are said to and, perhaps most importantly, that they refer not to a future hope but to a present reality: 'Today you will be with me in Paradise.' The term 'paradise' is so rich in meaning and so evocative down the ages. For us it refers to a place of beauty and peace, a new heaven and earth, a restored Eden, a recreated realm, a land of the blessed, a place to go to once we have died and where we see our loved ones again. In contrast, when Julian's understanding is lifted up, she does not so much see a place or realm but rather three heavens, the persons of the Trinity:

> And all in the blessed manhood of Christ, none is more, none is less, none is higher, none is lower but even alike in bliss.

Just as in her first revelation, when Julian, looking at Christ being crowned with a garland of thorns, was suddenly filled with joy by the Trinity and so realised that the whole Trinity was present with Christ on the cross, so now her delight and bliss at Christ's words lead her to a revelation of the presence of the three heavens within the person of Christ.

In many ways Julian's imagery follows Johannine theology, which is perfectly expressed in a very human moment in John's gospel, when Philip asks Jesus to 'show us the Father'. In response Jesus says, 'Whoever has seen me has seen the Father' (John 14:9). In the same way Julian only ever sees the Father through the Son. Christ is the human face of the Trinity, hence Julian always insists that the revelation of God's love and person can only be seen and known through the humanity of Christ. In this way, Julian goes against those who would call her a mystic in the sense of experiencing a mystical vision of the numinous nature of God. She does not seek to pierce the cloud of unknowing, to look behind the veil, to see God face to face in all his mystery. For Julian, the Father is seen and known in and through the person of Jesus Christ: 'I saw in Christ that the Father is.' This is enough for Julian.

Within the first heaven, Julian is therefore shown no bodily image of the Father, like a man seated on a throne as in the Carrow Psalter and other depictions of the throne of grace; rather, through the humanity of Christ, Julian has been given access to sight and knowledge of the intimate relationship of mutual love between the Father and the Son. Just as Julian and Christ's words reveal an intimate relationship of love and devotion in bodily terms, so now Julian has been given insight into the inner life of the Trinity and the bond of love that binds the three persons into one. It is this relationship which Julian sees as defining both the nature and the work of the Father:

> The work of the Father is this: that he gives a reward to his Son, Jesus Christ.

In the theology of the cross, we have moved from an act of love and reparation as expressed between Christ and Julian to the reward that the Father gives to the Son. This reward is so pleasing and so blessed to the Son that the Father could not have given him a gift that he could want or like more. So the first heaven is defined by the pleasure of the Father at all that Jesus has done on the cross and the reward that he gives him, which far surpasses the hard and shameful death he endured.

We are his crown

The gift and reward that the Father gives to the Son is a crown. In what seems like a staggering reversal of the first revelation, the crown of thorns, the instrument of torture and humiliation, has now been transformed into a crown of triumph and honour that resonates with the imagery of Revelation and Esdras, where those who have been faithful unto death are rewarded for their labours with the crown of life. But it is not that one crown, the crown of thorns, is simply replaced by another one of gold, the reward for his suffering. Julian's language and theology are more subtle and sublime than this. The key to Julian's understanding of what she sees is the nature of the crown itself:

> We be not only his by his dying, but also by the courteous gift of his Father we are his bliss, we are his reward, we are his worship, we are his crown – and this was a singular marvellous and a full delectable beholding that we are his crown.

The reward and gift that the Father gives the Son is us: the salvation, redemption and reconciliation of humanity to God. But the work of this reconciliation and the reward are not separate; they are one and the same thing. So the Son is no longer seen as being humiliated and mocked with a crown of thorns at his Passion, but rather this is the moment when he is crowned by the Father with a garland of thorns as his gift and reward for our bliss and joy.

We have travelled a long way through Julian's revelations of the Passion: from the garland of thorns, the retreating of Christ's face behind a curtain of dried blood and sin, to the pouring out of his life blood and long, slow dying, to this moment. In this journey Julian has taken us behind and beyond the veil of blood, the outer flesh and suffering of Christ to see within the inner life, love and purpose of the Trinity.

So we return to the garland of thorns, but we now see it with the eyes of the Trinity as the Son's crown of triumph and bliss, the salvation, bliss and joy of humanity. Thus, through Julian's writing we can truly say, as God's lovers like her, that we have learned to choose Jesus as our heaven, whom we have only seen in pain at this time.

Going deeper

Spend some time slowly reading and thinking about Julian's words:

> Then said our good Lord Jesus Christ, 'Are you well pleased that I suffered for you?' I said, "Yes, good Lord, gramercy. Yes, good Lord, blessed may you be!' Then said Jesus, our kind Lord: 'If you are pleased, I am pleased. It is a joy, a bliss, an endless pleasure to me that I ever suffered the Passion for you; and if I might suffer more, I would suffer more.' In this feeling my understanding was lifted up into heaven, and there I saw three heavens, of which sight I greatly marvelled.

What do these words say to you?

What do you find challenging and why?

What do you think Jesus would like to say to you?

Allow your time of thinking and reflecting to lead you into a deeper place of prayer and love.

What will you take away with you from this time of meditation?

Questions to ponder or discuss

- How do you understand the word 'heaven'?
- Who do you need to be reconciled with?
- What is the difference between forgiveness and reconciliation?
- How does Christ reconcile the world to God?
- How can you bring resurrection to a place or situation of despair?

Words for the journey

> In this is love, not that we loved God but that he loved us and sent his Son to be the atoning sacrifice for our sins.
>
> 1 JOHN 4:10

Conclusion

It took five years to diagnose. During that time, I learned that medicine is not so much a science, nor is it necessarily an art, but more often akin to detective work. Eventually, after the extraction of wisdom teeth, numerous appointments with eminent and highly skilled consultants, the culprit was named and set behind bars of medication. For the next ten years or so, living with the chronic pain condition called trigeminal neuralgia was a secret, hidden reality. Controlled mainly by medication, no one knew what was locked up behind closed doors. Only occasionally was I found curled up in a ball on my bed, paralysed by the excruciating pain that tore down my right cheek and jaw. Slowly and in gradual waves of time, the medication began to fail me. It could no longer be my bars of iron, my fire door which kept the flames of agony away. Eating became a trial, speaking a torture, but still I tried to hide it even as tears rolled down my cheek as I led another service and battled on through the pain.

Hope came in the form of a surgeon. For him the procedure was routine – but not for me, and so my secret had to come out, as the recovery period would take many months. The kindness, care and love of those around me was staggering. I had always been seen as the one who ministered to the sick and dying in the community, like some kind of angelic figure, robed in black, who appeared when needed. But now I was seen as just another person, one of humanity who suffers alongside and with others. Conversations about illness moved from moaning to real sharing and a silent understanding that needed no words. For what can words say when one is in agony? Only once did someone say to me, 'Well, you are lucky, you have your faith.' I didn't have the heart to tell them that when pain annihilates your being and consumes your world, there are no comfort blankets of faith. In that moment I did not think of the cross, or Jesus, or anything except the pain, and, in a state much like that of silent contemplation, just waited for it to pass. Even during the years of daily suffering, it didn't turn me to the cross to find comfort or an answer, because there was no simple answer, only suffering and endurance.

During those times I realise that when I could not pray, when pain had taken me beyond language and thought, I was in fact never alone. I was surrounded by an unseen cloud of witnesses, stretching back through time and space. Some I knew, but many I didn't, and they held me during my time of darkness. It was then that I really understood what the word 'church' means. It is a word so often belittled, abused and scoffed at today, but the church is simply people: some extraordinary but the majority very ordinary, unseen mostly and hidden in the crowd but known by their extraordinary acts and prayers. Their prayers did not ask for miracles or easy answers, but they stood with me, holding my hand, in silent solidarity. They are all God's true lovers who stand at the foot of the cross.

This was the place where Julian wanted to stand. She didn't realise what she was asking of Christ when she made her earnest request, but somehow she knew that the cross of Christ cannot be explained or understood through reason or learning. It is in and through our own suffering, when we silently hold the pain of another, when we patiently remain in the place of darkness, when we inhabit the place at the foot of the cross, that the darkness becomes our light.

Julian's writings offer us a revelation of divine love, and she speaks many beautiful and comfortable words that have been loved and valued over the years. But this book has not been about those words; instead it has focused on the heart of her revelation, which is a vision of the cross, and Julian's invitation to sit with her at its foot until we, like her, behold the cross, our own cross, the cross of others, the cross of the world, the cross of Christ as a revelation of divine love.

Further reading

Revelations of Divine Love – editions and translations

The Showings of Julian of Norwich, edited by Denise N. Baker, Norton Critical Edition (W.W. Norton & Co., 2005).

Julian of Norwich: Showings, edited and translated by Edmund Colledge and James Walsh, Classics of Western Spirituality Series (Paulist Press, 1978).

A Revelation of Divine Love, edited by Marion Glasscoe (Exeter University Press, 1986).

The Complete Julian of Norwich, translated by Father John-Julian, Paraclete Giants Series (Paraclete Press, 2009).

Julian of Norwich: Revelations of Divine Love, translated by Elizabeth Spearing (Penguin, 1998).

The Writings of Julian of Norwich: A vision showed to a devout woman and a revelation of love, edited by Nicholas Watson and Jacqueline Jenkins (The Pennsylvania State University Press, 2006).

Julian of Norwich: Revelations of Divine Love, edited by Barry Windeatt (Oxford University Press, 2016).

Julian of Norwich: Revelations of Divine Love, translated by Barry Windeatt, Oxford World Classics (Oxford University Press, 2015).

Studies in Julian

Abbott, Christopher, *Julian of Norwich: Autobiography and theology* (D.S. Brewer, 1999).

Baker, Denise, *Julian of Norwich's Showings: From vision to book* (Princeton University Press, 1994).

Fruehwirth, Robert, *The Drawing of this Love: Growing in faith with Julian of Norwich* (Canterbury Press, 2016).

Glasscoe, Marion, *English Medieval Mystics: Games of faith* (Longman, 1993).
Jantzen, Grace M., *Julian of Norwich: Mystic and theologian*, 2nd edition (SPCK, 2000).
Llewelyn, Robert (ed.), *Julian: Woman of our day* (DLT, 1985).
Llewelyn, Robert, *With Pity Not Blame: Reflections on the writings of Julian of Norwich and on The Cloud of Unknowing* (DLT, 1982).
Nuth, Joan, *Wisdom's Daughter: The theology of Julian of Norwich* (Crossroad, 1997).
Ramirez, Janina, *Julian of Norwich: A very brief history* (SPCK, 2016).
Rolf, Veronica Mary, *Julian's Gospel: Illuminating the life and revelations of Julian of Norwich* (Orbis Books, 2013).
Sheldrake, Philip, *Julian of Norwich: In God's sight* (Wiley Blackwell, 2018).
Turner, Denys, *Julian of Norwich: Theologian* (Yale University Press, 2011).
Upjohn, Sheila, *In Search of Julian of Norwich* (Darton, Longman and Todd, 1989).
Upjohn, Sheila, *Why Julian Now? A voyage of discovery* (Friends of Julian of Norwich, 2014).
Ward, Sister Benedicta, 'Julian the solitary', in *Julian Reconsidered* (SLG Press, 1988).

Praying with Julian

Durka, Gloria, *Praying with Julian of Norwich*, Companions for the Journey Series (Saint Mary's Press, 2001).
Gruchy, Isobel de, *Making All Things Well: Finding spiritual strength with Julian of Norwich* (Paulist Press, 2013).
Nelson, John (ed.), *Julian of Norwich: Journeys into joy – selected spiritual writings* (New City Press, 2001).
Lewin, Ann, *Love is the Meaning: Growing in faith with Julian of Norwich* (Canterbury Press, 2006).

Novels about Julian

Coles, Margaret, *The Greening* (Hay House, 2013).
Parke, Simon, *The Secret Testament of Julian* (White Crow Books, 2018).

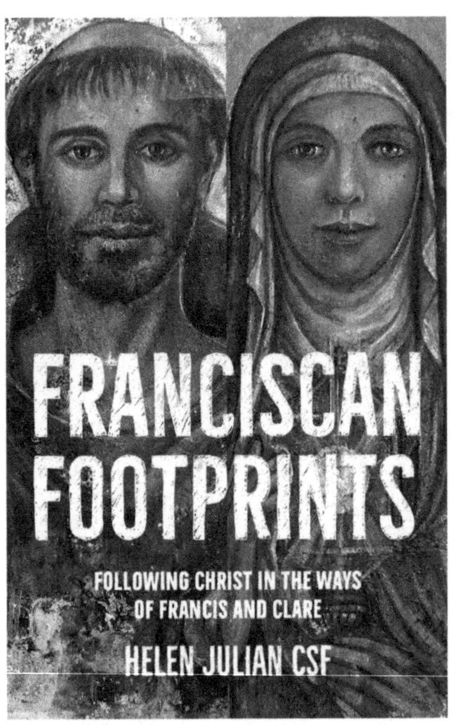

There are many ways of following Christ – each footprint is unique. One of these, the Franciscan spiritual journey, has been tried and tested over the centuries, and the experiences of St Francis and St Clare and all those who have been inspired by their lives still resonate with us. Helen Julian CSF explores the distinctive features of their spirituality and shows how these practices can be applied to, and become part of, our daily lives. Through stories of care for creation, social justice, mission, preaching, contemplative spirituality and simple living, discover your own pathway today.

Franciscan Footprints
Following Christ in the ways of Francis and Clare
Helen Julian
978 0 85746 811 6 £8.99

brfonline.org.uk

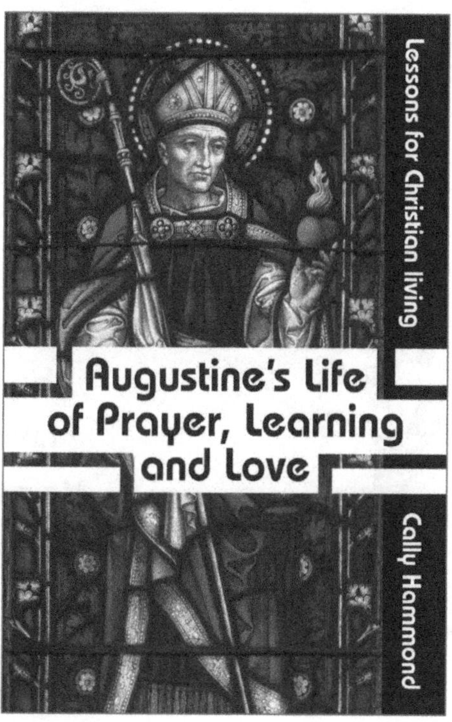

There are many books that tell the life story of Augustine and how he has been fundamental in shaping western Christian theology and practice. This is not one of them. This book is about how he became a Christian – the problems he faced; the doubts he struggled with. It is about how he made sense of his belief in God and shared it with other people. It is about how he learned to read the Bible and to pray. And it is about the word which is at the heart of his Christian life – love. It concludes with moments of prayer from Augustine's life, in which he glimpses visions of God, encouraging the reader to take their own next steps in discipleship.

Augustine's Life of Prayer, Learning and Love
Lessons for Christian living
Cally Hammond
978 0 85746 713 3 £8.99

brfonline.org.uk

Enabling all ages to grow in faith

Anna Chaplaincy
Barnabas in Schools
Holy Habits
Living Faith
Messy Church
Parenting for Faith

The Bible Reading Fellowship (BRF) is a Christian charity that resources individuals and churches and provides a professional education service to primary schools.

Our vision is to enable people of all ages to grow in faith and understanding of the Bible and to see more people equipped to exercise their gifts in leadership and ministry.

To find out more about our ministries and programmes, visit

brf.org.uk